STOCKWELL-MUDD LIBRARIES
PS614.M45
Poetry of to-day

3 5044 00248 1759

POETRY OF TO-DAY

AN ANTHOLOGY

EDITED BY

ROSA M. R. MIKELS

AND

GRACE SHOUP

INSTRUCTORS IN THE DEPARTMENT OF ENGLISH
SHORTRIDGE HIGH SCHOOL, INDIANAPOLIS

CHARLES SCRIBNER'S SONS

NEW YORK   CHICAGO   BOSTON
ATLANTA   SAN FRANCISCO

Copyright, 1927, by
CHARLES SCRIBNER'S SONS

Printed in the United States of America
B

PS
614
.MH5

113204

INTRODUCTION

Do you like to go adventuring? If you do, you will like the new poetry. It offers adventures in travel, for it will take you to the Santa Fé Trail, to the heights of the Sierras, to the farms of the Middle West, to lovely yet austere New England, to the fairy-haunted hills of Ireland, to the Most-Sacred Mountain of China, where Confucius once stood, and to mysterious Bagdad. And it offers adventures in friendship with all kinds of people, among them the miner, the farmer, the telephone girl, the oriental merchant. It also invites adventure in discovering beauty and truth, as these are understood by the world to-day.

You may ask, "Why call this the *new* poetry?" Of course it is new in the obvious way that a garment or a house may be new; that is, recently made. But it is new in the profounder sense that Chaucer's poetry was new in his day; Shakespeare's was new; Wordsworth's and Byron's and Keats's was new. These men spoke to the people of their own day on topics that keenly interested them, and they interpreted the world in language and symbols that every one could understand. Always there are the many who are inarticulate when they try to comprehend nature and life, and the poet helps them to become vocal. He says what they feel but cannot express.

The poetry of to-day is marked by simplicity and sincerity. There are, of course, many who write pretty verse in a pretty way, and they have their admirers. But the worth-while poetry of either past or present is a genuine outpouring of emotion. The heart overflows in the presence of some object or in the contemplation of some truth. Nothing that really appeals to the poet is unworthy. So in this volume you will find poems about excavations, cabbages, tea, sky-scrapers, automobiles, and Saturday night crowds in large cities; blossoms, rivers, sunsets, mountains, and sea—themes that have always appealed to poets; and the age-old problems of love and life. Sincerity in dealing with them is the indispensable thing.

But this sincerity demands not only that the poet feel the worth of his subject, but that he use language which is natural to him and his readers, the language in which he and they think and speak. Chaucer chose his words thus, although his English seems to us strange and difficult; and thus spoke the true poets after Chaucer. If the language of their day was good enough for them, so is the language of the present good enough for us. Therefore our poets have largely given up the diction that was once regarded as essential to poetry. They say "over," not "o'er"; "girl," not "maiden," "damsel," or "the fair"; they talk of "eyes" instead of "orbs"; and such forms as "thou," "thee," and "hast" they seldom use, although these were once common in speech and suited to the time of their use. Even in speaking of God, the poet is quite likely to say "You" instead of "Thou" and to say it very reverently, too.

The poet's desire to be sincere and true to himself also extends to the form of his poem. If he feels like using an old form, if it is suited to his mood and theme, he uses it. But he will not torture his ideas into conventional meters and rhythms if he can find those that express him better, and he is quite indifferent to the complaints of conservatives that "Longfellow and Tennyson never wrote that way." The new forms which the modern poet has devised for his better expression have found—as might have been expected—imitators who have written some very indifferent prose which they have labelled "poetry" and which they have measured off by some metrical yardstick of their own manufacture. But it is not of these we speak when we talk of the poets of to-day.

The new poetry talks a good deal about cadences. These

may be defined as the phrase rhythms of nature and ordinary speech. The cadence pause is one of the effective devices of poetry, old or new. A group of words may not be especially effective by itself, but set it in a line of poetry and break it with a cadence pause, and it may reveal beauty. "The love of those who were older" is not especially beautiful as a group of words, but when Poe breaks it with a cadence pause, he creates a beauty of sound that we recognize as poetry and as a suitable means of expressing his thought:

> "But our love it was stronger by far than the love
>   Of those who were older than we,
>   Of many far wiser than we . . . "

As to the cadences of speech, every people and every age probably has its own. John Erskine says in his essay, "The New Poetry" (1920): "The cadence of American speech is no longer the same as that of English, and it was from the English models that the best American poets fifty years ago learned the cadence both of their speech and of their verse; it is not surprising, therefore, that to the American ear of to-day the fall of Tennyson's line, or Lowell's, or Longfellow's, sounds strange, almost foreign. Our average fellow citizen speaks more directly now, with less subtlety and also with less delay. Our conversation is a succession of hammer-strokes, not links of sweetness long drawn out. Whether or not we approve, this is the fact, and we need not wonder that a people whose talk is such should ask for a verse which preserves, in however elevated a form, the same fashion of discourse."

Then there are the cadences of nature, which the poet discovers. The movements of water, the blowing of the wind over prairies or through the wet needles of the pines are illustrations.

If a cadence is often repeated, it may form the pattern— to use a modern term—of the poem. But the writer will vary the cadence in order that it may give us renewed pleasure when he uses it again. A striking instance of this use of cadence is to be found in Amy Lowell's "Patterns." Its cadences are indicated in the notes on that poem.

But the writer does not always depend on cadences for the pattern of his poem. He may use rhythm, which is the undulation of his line, or rhyme—both of which are familiar in the poetry of the past as well as in the poetry of to-day. Or the pattern may be that often employed in the Bible, parallelism, in which the thought is repeated with variety in wording or figure:

> "The waters are hid as with a stone,
>   And the face of the deep is frozen."
>   Job 38:30

Again the poet may use image or symbol, or resort to such devices as free verse or polyphonic prose.

If the image is the device used, the writer insists on the exact word in order that the image communicated may be clear and distinct. By the exact word he means the one most closely expressing or describing the thing mentioned, the action that occurred, or the condition that existed. The image is the picture or concept conveyed to the reader's mind by the poem read. Precision is the aim of the "imagist." Let us contrast Keats's "Ode to Autumn" with Carl Sandburg's description of an Illinois farmer harvesting his corn.

Keats says to personified Autumn:

> "Who hath not seen thee oft amid thy store?
>   Sometimes whoever seeks abroad may find
> Thee sitting careless on a granary floor,
>   Thy hair soft-lifted by the winnowing wind;
> Or on a half-reap'd furrow sound asleep,
>   Drows'd with the fumes of poppies, while thy hook
>   Spares the next swath and all its twined flowers:
> And sometimes like a gleaner thou dost keep
>   Steady thy laden head across a brook;
>   Or by a cider-press, with patient look,
>   Thou watchest the last oozings, hours by hours."

Carl Sandburg is content to show us the Illinois farmers at their work:

> " . . . . the farmers husked their
> corn in the old-fashioned Studebaker wagons:
> the cream and gold ears sent a shine
> between the green wagon boards, over the tops
> of the green wagon boards, . . ."

There is beauty in Keats's classic and traditional images and a superlative beauty of sound in his warm, dragging cadences. He has shown us the languorous drowsiness of autumnal days as through a many-colored glass. But the scene he describes is not like that in America, when the farmers hurry to get in their crop. Sandburg has been true to what he has seen and has given us the exact image of the "cream and gold ears" that "sent a shine between the green wagon boards."

Symbols have always been used by poets. Note the prophet Isaiah:

> "Ho, every one that thirsteth,
> come ye to the waters,
> and he that hath no money;
> come ye, buy and eat;
> yea, come,
> buy wine and milk,
> without money and without price."

This, of course, is a call to salvation veiled under oriental symbolism. A. D. Waley translates a little Japanese "tanka" (a poem of five lines), in which the symbolism concerns a fickle girl:

> "O cuckoo,
> Because the villages where you sing
> Are so many,
> I am estranged from you, even
> In the midst of my love!"

Adelaide Crapsey's "Cinquains," Alfred Kreymborg's "Old Manuscript," and William Rose Benét's "The Falconer of

God" are striking examples of symbolism. A few lines from Vachel Lindsay's long poem, "The Congo," illustrate the effectiveness of the sudden introduction of the symbol:

> "Death is an Elephant,
> Torch-eyed and horrible,
> Foam-flanked and terrible."

Something should be said about free verse, or *vers libre*, and polyphonic prose. Writers of free verse have shown that beautiful cadences may produce poetry without recourse to any fixed metrical scheme: and they have made vigorous use of harsh cadences to express harsh situations or crude power, as in Carl Sandburg's "Chicago." The irregular lines and the frequent disregard for the conventional use of capitals at the beginning of lines sometimes shock the unaccustomed eye; but the rhythms and cadences less frequently offend the ear. Polyphonic prose is printed in paragraphs, like prose, but makes free use of assonance, alliteration, rhyme, and other poetic devices.

The new poetry is generally dated from Walt Whitman, who was the first to show that a new land with vast spaces, unbounded energies, and untold possibilities need not follow the Old World in its themes and patterns for poetry. The French were prompt to recognize greatness in the new rhythms of Whitman, so rough and formless to the ear of his day. The poets of Ireland felt the influence not only of Celtic tradition but of the *vers libre* of France, stimulated by Whitman; and thus through France, Ireland, and England, the stream of the Whitman influence turned back home.

But other influences than Whitman's have been at work to make the poetry of to-day different from that of the past. America has felt the influence of other nations, other races. European peoples, Africa, the islands of the sea, China, Persia, Japan, and India have contributed to our music, our graphic arts, our architecture, and our literature. Moreover the American poets have discovered in a true sense their country. Its spaciousness, its diversity of scenes and people, and its historic interest have captured their imagination. Therefore each section has its poet-interpreters, as a little study of the biographies in this book will show.

Best of all, the poet of to-day has discovered the charm of the commonplace. He finds in life as it is lived by ordinary people beauty and significance. It fascinates him if he can find in it virility and sincerity, even when it is coarse and harsh.

These contacts with peoples of different blood, made possible by our conglomerate population, this interest in his own environment, and this splendid and childlike curiosity about the common things of life have developed in our poets an all-inclusive love for humanity. Hard workers themselves, they sympathize with those who toil. Having claimed mental and spiritual freedom for themselves, they want to secure it for others, to remove inequalities that make men enemies instead of brothers. As John Hall Wheelock says, they would

> "Trample them with love,
> Ride over them with love."

An inclusive anthology of modern verse in the English language must contain three types of verse: poetry written in England by Masefield, de la Mare, Gibson, and others; Irish poetry written in English with a haunting Celtic undertone; and poetry written in America, some of which might have been written in England or Ireland, and some of which is very different from poetry in English that is written elsewhere—except that several of the most distinctive of the American Imagists now make their homes in England, where they are still considered typically American.

The rise of every new school of art is a criticism of the faults that have grown up among the imitators of past excellences. It is not destructive of the true beauty of the past nor unappreciative of its best qualities. New forms of verse in no way displace the old; they only add to man's possessions in the realms of beauty. It is a far cry from Chaucer to Sandburg, but there is beauty all the way—and beyond.

NOTES ON VERSIFICATION

METERS

The feet, or sound groups, most commonly used in English verse are the iamb or iambus, the trochee, the anapest, and the dactyl. The adjectives derived from these nouns are iambic, trochaic, anapestic, dactylic. When two of these feet occur in one line the measure is called dimeter; when three occur, we call the measure trimeter; four make tetrameter; five, pentameter; six, hexameter; seven, heptameter.

Feet are composed of recurrent stressed syllables, accompanied by a varied number of unstressed syllables. These are usually referred to in rhetorics as long and short syllables, and as that is a convenient terminology, it will be used here.

The iambus is short, long; ∪—

The trochee is long, short;— ∪

The anapest is short, short, long; ∪ ∪—

The dactyl is long, short, short;— ∪ ∪

The spondee is made up of two equally accented syllables, long, long;— —. This foot is common in Greek and Roman verse, but many students of English feel that its place is taken in our strongly stressed language by the trochee and the iambus.

RHYME AND ASSONANCE

In English poetry rhyme is commonly used as a melodious device except in blank verse, and sometimes in free verse.

Rhyme may be defined as an identity of the vowel sound in the last accented syllable, and an absolute identity of all sounds following it. These identical accented vowels must be preceded by different consonant sounds.

A rhyme of one syllable only, *cry* and *sigh*, is called a single or masculine rhyme. A rhyme of two syllables, *beauty* and *duty*, is called a double or feminine rhyme. A rhyme of three syllables, *astrology* and *geology* is called a triple rhyme.

The terminal rhyme, or end rhyme, is most common; but one finds also the frequent use of internal rhyme, as in Tennyson's "The Revenge":

"And the stately Spanish men to their flag-ship bore him then,
   Where they laid him by the mast, old Sir Richard caught at
     last,
   And they praised him to his face with their courtly foreign
     grace."

Closely related to rhyme are the repetition of vowel sounds, or assonance, and the repetition of consonant sounds, or alliteration. Both are seen in these lines from Poe's "Raven":

"And the silken sad uncertain rustling of each purple curtain
   Thrilled me, filled me, with fantastic terrors never felt be-
     fore."

We find the sound "ur" in "certain," "purple," and "curtain," the sound "il" in "silken," "filled," and "thrilled." A long study might be made of the use of consonant sounds in these two lines where the liquid "l's" and "r's" suggest the richness of the curtains and the unquiet "s" and "t" and "f," repeated again and again, suggest uneasiness and fear.

THE STANZA

"The stanza is the unit," says Brander Matthews, "of which the sequence constitutes the poem." Most stanzas of the classic types are recognized by the eye and ear by the arrangement of rhymes, and the meter.

Whittier's "Maud Muller" is an example of the use of the couplet (aa).

> "Beneath her torn hat glowed the wealth
> Of simple beauty and rustic health."

Browning's "A Toccata of Galuppi's" is written in triplets (aaa).

> "Here you come with your old music, and here's all the good
>   it brings;
> What, they lived once thus at Venice where the merchants
>   were the kings,
> Where St. Mark's is, where the Doges used to wed the sea
>   with rings?"

The quatrain is by far the commonest stanza in English. Often the first and third lines rhyme together and the second and fourth (abab) as in Emerson's

> "So nigh is grandeur to our dust,
>   So near is God to Man,
> When Duty whispers low, 'Thou must,'
>   The Youth replies, 'I can.' "

This form is often used, but the first and third lines may be left unrhymed, the second and fourth only rhyming. Then again, a quatrain may be simply two couplets, the first and second and the third and fourth lines rhyming together (aabb). In Tennyson's "In Memoriam," the first and fourth and the second and third lines rhyme (a b b a). In Fitzgerald's translation of the "Rubaiyat," the first and second lines rhyme with the fourth, and the third is unrhymed (a a—a).

> "They say the lion and the lizard keep
> The courts where Jamshyd gloried and drank deep,
> And Bahram, that great hunter—the wild ass
> Stamps o'er his head but cannot break his sleep."

In five-line stanzas we find many variations of two lines rhyming together, while the other three employ another rhyme (such as, a a a b b; a b a b a; a a b b b). Longfellow's "The Village Blacksmith" is an example of the six-line stanza which has but three rhymed lines (—a, —a, —a). Other six-line stanzas have two alternate rhymes (a b a b a b); others have three couplets (a a b b c c); still others have a quatrain and a couplet (a b a b c c).

In Holmes's "The Last Leaf," Longfellow's "The Cumberland," and Burns's "To a Mountain Daisy" we find other variations. An eight-line stanza may be a six-line stanza followed by a couplet, as in "Don Juan," but is more likely to be two successive quatrains tied together by the repetition of one rhyme. The ten-line stanza permits many arrangements. Gray's "Elegy" is one example, but probably no arrangement of rhymes in this stanza is forbidden by precedent. One of the most delightfully musical stanzas in English is the Spenserian, eight iambic pentameter lines followed by a ninth in iambic hexameter, and with a rhyme-scheme which may be represented by a b a b b c b c c, Spenser's "Faerie Queene," Keats's "The Eve of St. Agnes," and Shelley's "Adonais," and many other beautiful poems are written in this stanza.

Imported from the French are certain fixed poem-forms, the rondel, the rondeau, the triolet, the villanelle, the ballade, and the chant-royal. Austin Dobson and Algernon Swinburne were master-workers in these forms. The foremost fixed poem-form in English, the sonnet, came to us from the Italian, but has been at home in our language for three hundred years. The sonnet is complete in itself. It is a stanza of fourteen iambic pentameter lines, expressing a single lofty thought or emotion, preferably in an arrangement of eight and six lines. The first two quatrains, or eight lines, develop the thought; the six concluding lines reflect on the thought developed in the first eight. The accepted rhyme-scheme for the quatrains is a b b a a b b a. One of two rhyme-schemes is preferred for the sestette, or concluding six lines, with either c d e c d e or c d c d c d. Many noble sonnets have varied slightly from this form. Shakespeare's form was three quatrains followed by a couplet.

Most epic poetry in English is written in unrhymed iambic pentameter. This is called blank verse. "Evangeline" is written in unrhymed dactylic hexameter. Epic poems are not divided into stanzas but into sections called "books." An unrhymed metrical couplet is called a distich. In the eighteenth century Pope was the foremost exponent of the use of the heroic couplet in long narratives:—iambic pentameter lines rhyming in pairs and scrupulously observing a pause in each line, called the cæsura.

In much of the verse of to-day we find marked evidence of the influence of the old ballads or folk poetry of the English and the Scotch. The typical ballad measure, as in "Sir Patrick Spens," "Glasgerion," and the Robin Hood ballads, was composed in iambic quatrains with four feet in the first and third lines, and three in the second and fourth lines, which carried the rhyme. The meter was

$$U—, \ U—, \ U—, \ U—,$$
$$U—, \ U—, \ U—,$$

and the rhyme-scheme was usually —a—a; but it is not so much the meter of the ballad as several of its conventions— the question and answer, the refrain, the suggestion of the supernatural, and the simplicity of the diction—that influences the poet of to-day.

Free verse is dealt with at greater length in the introduction.

ACKNOWLEDGMENTS

For permission to use selections in this book we are indebted to the following: D. Appleton & Company for "On the Great Plateau" by Edith Wyatt; *The Argonaut* for "A White Iris" by Pauline B. Barrington; Barse & Hopkins for "Fleurette" by Robert W. Service; Bobbs-Merrill Company for "The Heart of the Bugle" by Meredith Nicholson, "A Life Lesson," "A Parting Guest," and "When the Frost Is On the Punkin" by James Whitcomb Riley; Boni & Liveright for "Priapus" and "Oread" by H. D.; Brandt and Brandt for "When the Year Grows Old" by Edna St. Vincent Millay from "Renascence and Other Poems," published by Harper & Brothers, copyright, 1917, by Edna St. Vincent Millay; Burns, Oates & Washbourne, Ltd., for "Lepanto" by G. K. Chesterton; Joseph Campbell for "The Old Woman"; Jonathan Cape, Ltd., for "Nature's Friend" by W. H. Davies; The Century Company for "The Runner in the Skies" by James Oppenheim; Florence Earle Coates for "The Unconquered Air"; *Contemporary Verse* for "Won by Ear" by Daniel Troy and "To Think" by Elizabeth Coatsworth; Alice Corbin for "What Dim Arcadian Pastures"; Dodd, Mead & Company for "May Is Building Her House" by Richard Le Gallienne, "The House of Christmas" and "The Donkey" by G. K. Chesterton, "The Soldier" by Rupert Brooke, "The Toy Band" by Sir Henry Newbolt, and "Our Little House" by Thomas Walsh; George H. Doran Company for "Trees" by Joyce Kilmer and "Song Against Children" by Aline Kilmer; E. P. Dutton & Company for "America the Beautiful" and "Yellow Warblers" by Katharine Lee Bates, "Everyone Sings" by Siegfried Sassoon, "The Spires of Oxford" by Winifred M. Letts, "The Common Street" by Helen Gray Cone, and "Return" by Willard Wattles; *Everybody's Magazine* for "Shade" and "The Ballad of the Cross" by Theodosia Garrison; John Finley for "The Red Cross Spirit Speaks"; Hildegarde Flanner for "To a Tree in Bloom" and "Daphne"; James Elroy Flecker for "The Golden Journey to Samarkand"; John Gould Fletcher for "Spring" and "Arizona"; Ford Madox Ford for "Old Houses of Flanders"; The Four Seas Company for "The Poplar" by Richard Aldington; Harcourt, Brace & Company for "Caliban in the Coal Mines" by Louis Untermeyer and "Haunted" by Wilbert Snow; Harper & Brothers for "The Melancholy Beaver" by Arthur Guiterman; Henry Holt & Company for "Birches," "Mending Wall," and "The Sound of the Trees" by Robert Frost, "Fog," "Monotone," "Sheep," and "Child" by Carl Sandburg, "Miss Loo," "The Listeners," and "Silver" by Walter de la Mare, "An Old Woman of the Roads" by Padraic Colum, and "Sweetwater Range" by Lew Sarett; Houghton Mifflin Company for "The House and the Road" and "The Cedars" by Josephine Preston Peabody, "Refugees" and "After Sunset" by Grace Conkling, "Little Gray Songs" by Grace F. Norton, "My Wage" by Jessie Rittenhouse, "Music I Heard" by Conrad Aiken, "In Lady Street" and "The Feckenham Men" by John Drinkwater, "A Lady," "Patterns," and "Red Slippers" by Amy Lowell, "Her Words" by Anna Hempstead Branch, and "The Automobile" by Percy Mackaye; B. W. Huebsch for "Autumn" by Jean Starr Untermeyer; *The Independent* for "The Fisherman's Tax" by Grace Shoup; Mary Johnston for "Virginiana"; Mitchell Kennerley for "I Am in Love with High Far-Seeing Places" and "I Am Weary of Being Bitter" by Henry Davison Ficke, and "I Am the Wind" by Zoë Akins; Alfred A. Knopf for "To a Phoebe Bird" and "The Fields" by Witter Bynner, "The Palatine" by Willa Cather, "Dance Figure" by Ezra Pound, "Coming to Port" and "At the Aquarium" by Max Eastman, "The Most Sacred Mountain" by Eunice Tietjens, "Saturday Night" by James Oppenheim, "Old Manuscript" by Alfred Kreymborg, "November Night" and "Fate Defied" by Adelaide Crapsey; Richard Le Gallienne for "A Caravan from China Comes" and "A Ballade-Catalogue of Lovely Things"; Little, Brown & Company for "A Day" by Emily Dickinson, and "The Miner" by Richard Burton; The Macmillan Company for "Souls" by Fannie Stearns Davis, "Harbury" by Louise Driscoll, "A Chant Out-of-Doors" and "Ghosts" by Marguerite Wilkinson, "The Lonely Tree" and "The Orphans" by Wilfrid Wilson Gibson, "Cargoes" and "Sea-Fever" by John Masefield, "Pocahontas" and "The Santa Fé Trail" by Vachel Lindsay, "Stupidity Street" by Ralph Hodgson, "Departure" by Hermann Hagedorn, "The Fountain" and "Barter" by Sara Teasdale, "Goethals" by Percy Mackaye, "The Sleeping Beauty" by Mary Carolyn Davies, "The Song of the Wandering Ængus" and "The Fiddler of Dooney" by William Butler Yeats, "The Pine at Timberline" and "On the Porch" by Harriet Monroe, "Isaiah Beethoven" and "Anne Rutledge" by Edgar Lee Masters, "Real Property" by Harold Monro; Edwin Markham for "The Man with the Hoe" and "Lincoln, the Man of the People"; Wilfred Meynell for "The Shepherdess" by Alice Meynell; Moffat, Yard & Company for "The Herd Boy" by Haniel Long; Thomas B. Mosher Company for "Frost To-Night" by Edith Thomas, "Sometimes" by Thomas S. Jones, Jr., "A Christmas Folk-Song" by Lizette Woodworth Reese; The Nation for "Standards" by Charles W. Stork; The New Republic for "The Excavation" by Max Endicoff; The New York Times for "The Message" by Dorothy Leonard; The Outlook Company for "The Sisters" by Louise A. Garnett; L. C. Page & Company for "Lord of My Heart's Elation" by Bliss Carman; Poetry for "The Harp of the Wind," "Who Loves the Rain," and "Cologne Cathedral" by Frances Shaw; G. P. Putnam's Sons for "In Flanders Fields" by John McCrae, and "Each In His Own Tongue" by William H. Carruth; Reilly & Lee Company for "Laddies" by Edgar A. Guest; Cale Young Rice for "The Mystic"; A. M. Robertson for "The Black Vulture" by George Sterling; Clinton Scollard for "As I Came Down from Lebanon"; Charles Scribner's Sons for "The City Dweller" by Bernice Kenyon, "I Have a Rendezvous with Death" by Alan Seeger, "Vive la France!" by Charlotte Holmes Crawford, "The Bells of Peace" by John Galsworthy, "The Lion House" and "Love and Liberation" by John Hall Wheelock, "Stains" by Theodosia Garrison, "Little Boy Blue" by Eugene Field, "The House on the Hill" and "Miniver Cheevy" by Edwin Arlington Robinson, "Work" by Henry van Dyke, "The Path Flower" by Olive Tilford Dargan, "A Ballad of Trees and the Master" by Sidney Lanier; Constance Lindsay Skinner for "Song of the Full Catch"; Small, Maynard & Company for "The Grave Digger" by Bliss Carman and "The Sea Gypsy" by Richard Hovey; The Sonnet for "The Old Plough Horse" by M. L. Fisher; The Spectator for "A Prayer for a Little Home" by Florence Bone; Frederick A. Stokes Company for "Ghosts of the New World" and "Princeton" by Alfred Noyes; The Sun for "God, You Have Been Too Good to Me" by Charles W. Stork; John Curtis Underwood for "Central"; University of California Chronicle for "Poplar Trees are Happiest" by John Russell McCarthy; A. P. Watt & Sons for "The Way Through the Wood" by Rudyard Kipling and "The Making of Birds" and "Sheep and Lambs" by Katharine Tynan Hinkson; James T. White & Company for "Canticle" by William Griffith; G. E. Woodberry for "Comrades"; Yale University Press for "Parenthood" and "Wish" by John C. Farrar, "Good Company" by Karle Wilson Baker, "The Falconer of God" and "Woolworth Tower" by William Rose Benét; Doubleday, Page & Company for "O to Make the Most Jubilant Poem," from "Leaves of Grass" by Walt Whitman.

CONTENTS

THE OUT-OF-DOORS

WAR, PATRIOTISM, AND PEACE

THE SEA AND ADVENTURE

CONTENTS

GOD AND MYSTERIES

LIFE AND LOVE

AMERICA

LABOR AND DEMOCRACY

PORTRAITS AND FANCIES

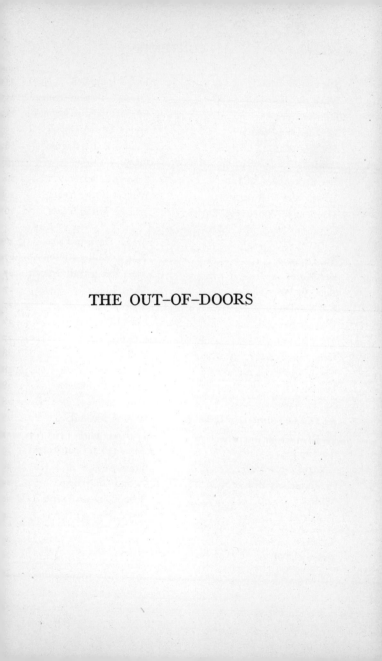

THE OUT-OF-DOORS

O TO MAKE THE MOST JUBILANT POEM

Walt Whitman was born at West Hills, Long Island, 1819. His father was of English ancestry, and his mother was Dutch. He attended school in Brooklyn till he was thirteen. After that he was a printer, a country school-teacher, a writer, an editor, a carpenter—whatever came to his hand was good. When he was about thirty he took, as did Vachel Lindsay after him, a joyous tramp-like tour through the Middle West, the Farther West, and the South. He served as a nurse in the army hospitals in the Civil War. Later he had a desk in the Department of the Interior. He died at his brother's home in Brooklyn, 1892.

O to make the most jubilant poem!
Even to set off these, and merge with these, the carol of death.
O full of music! full of manhood, womanhood, and infancy!
Full of common employments, full of grain and trees.
O for the voice of animals! O for the swiftness and balance
      of fishes!
O for the dropping of rain-drops in a poem!
O for the sunshine, and the motion of waves in a poem!

WALT WHITMAN

A CHANT OUT-OF-DOORS

Marguerite Wilkinson was born in Halifax, Nova Scotia, and educated in the Township High School, Evanston, Illinois, at the Misses Ely's School, and at Northwestern University.   She was the editor of "New Voices," a well-known anthology, and the author of several volumes of poetry.   She died in 1928.

"A Chant Out-of-Doors" has two interlocking rhythms, each expressing a mood of its own: the first is a jubilant worship; the second a meditation on the reasons for worship.   The writer suggests that the poem can be used antiphonally.

God of grave nights,
God of brave mornings,
God of silent noon,
Hear my salutation!

For where the rapids rage white and scornful,
I have passed safely, filled with wonder;
Where the sweet pools dream under willows,
I have been swimming, filled with life.

God of round hills,
God of green valleys,
God of clear springs,
Hear my salutation!

For where the moose feeds, I have eaten berries,
Where the moose drinks, I have drunk deep.
When the storm crashed through broken heavens—
And under clear skies—I have known joy.

God of great trees,
God of wild grasses,

God of little flowers,
Hear my salutation!

   For where the deer crops and the beaver plunges,
   Near the river I have pitched my tent;
   Where the pines cast aromatic needles
   On a still floor, I have known peace.

God of grave nights,
God of brave mornings,
God of silent noon,
Hear my salutation!

                 MARGUERITE WILKINSON

BIRCHES

Robert Frost was born in San Francisco of Yankee parentage.
He was taken to New England at the age of ten. His most noted
book, "North of Boston," tells of New England farm folk. He
has attended Dartmouth and Harvard and taught in Amherst.
His first recognition as a poet of the first rank was received in
England, where he lived for several years. He is now living on
a farm in Vermont.

"Birches" is a talking poem rather than a singing poem. Indeed, the author speaks to us at times with almost startling
directness. We enjoy his strong verbs and his fidelity to details;
for instance, the "click" of ice-bent boughs, the "crystal shells"
heaped beneath the trees. The poem has in it autobiographical
touches, revealing the "boy who could play alone" and the man
who found life "too much like a pathless wood." The concluding lines tell how he would spend his later years, climbing

> "Toward heaven till the tree could bear no more,
> But dipped its top and set me down again."

When I see birches bend to left and right
Across the line of straighter darker trees,
I like to think some boy's been swinging them.
But swinging doesn't bend them down to stay.
Ice-storms do that. Often you must have seen them
Loaded with ice a sunny winter morning
After a rain. They click upon themselves
As the breeze rises, and turn many-colored
As the stir cracks and crazes their enamel.
Soon the sun's warmth makes them shed crystal shells
Shattering and avalanching on the snow-crust—
Such heaps of broken glass to sweep away
You'd think the inner dome of heaven had fallen.
They are dragged to the withered bracken by the load,
And they seem not to break; though, once they are bowed

So low for long, they never right themselves:
You may see their trunks arching in the woods
Years afterward, trailing their leaves on the ground
Like girls on hands and knees that throw their hair
Before them over their heads to dry in the sun.
But I was going to say when Truth broke in
With all her matter-of-fact about the ice-storm
I should prefer to have some boy bend them
As he went out and in to fetch the cows—
Some boy too far from town to learn baseball,
Whose only play was what he found himself,
Summer or winter, and could play alone.
One by one he subdued his father's trees
By riding them down over and over again
Until he took the stiffness out of them,
And not one but hung limp, not one was left
For him to conquer. He learned all there was
To learn about not launching out too soon
And so not carrying the tree away
Clear to the ground. He always kept his poise
To the top branches, climbing carefully
With the same pains you use to fill a cup
Up to the brim, and even above the brim.
Then he flung outward, feet first, with a swish,
Kicking his way down through the air to the ground.

So was I once myself a swinger of birches;
And so I dream of going back to be.
It's when I'm weary of considerations,
And life is too much like a pathless wood
Where your face burns and tickles with the cobwebs
Broken across it, and one eye is weeping
From a twig's having lashed across it open.

I'd like to get away from earth awhile
And then come back to it and begin over.

May no fate wilfully misunderstand me
And half grant what I wish and snatch me away
Not to return. Earth's the right place for love:
I don't know where it's likely to go better.
I'd like to go by climbing a birch-tree,
And climb black branches up a snow-white trunk
Toward heaven, till the tree could bear no more,
But dipped its top and set me down again.
That would be good both going and coming back.
One could do worse than be a swinger of birches.

ROBERT FROST

TREES

Joyce Kilmer was born at New Brunswick, New Jersey. He was educated at Rutgers College and Columbia. Only a few days after America entered the World War he enlisted as a private in the Seventh Regiment of the National Guard, New York. He was killed in action, July 30, 1918.

I think that I shall never see
A poem lovely as a tree.

A tree whose hungry mouth is prest
Against the earth's sweet flowing breast;

A tree that looks at God all day,
And lifts her leafy arms to pray;

A tree that may in summer wear
A nest of robins in her hair;

Upon whose bosom snow has lain;
Who intimately lives with rain.

Poems are made by fools like me,
But only God can make a tree.

JOYCE KILMER

THE WAY THROUGH THE WOODS

Rudyard Kipling was born in Bombay, India. He was educated in England, but was working on a newspaper in India when the power of his short stories first startled the world. He is one of the most vigorous and prolific writers of our time, whether in prose or verse. He won the Nobel Prize for Literature in 1907. He lived for a brief time in Vermont, but has lived for many years in England. His only son was lost in the World War.

In "The Way Through the Woods" the tremendous power of Nature to obliterate traces of man's occupancy is suggested. But there is also a haunting suggestion of presences that still know and use the path through the wood—"But there is no road through the woods!"

They shut the road through the woods
Seventy years ago.
Weather and rain have undone it again,
And now you would never know
There was once a road through the woods
Before they planted the trees.
It is underneath the coppice and heath,
And the thin anemones.
Only the keeper sees
That, where the ring-dove broods,
And the badger rolls at ease,
There was once a way through the woods.

Yet, if you enter the woods
Of a summer evening late,
When the night air cools on the trout-ringed pools
Where the otter whistles his mate,
(They fear not men in the woods,
Because they see so few)

You will hear the beat of a horse's feet,
And the swish of a skirt in the dew,
Steadily cantering through
The misty solitudes,
As though they perfectly knew
The old lost road through the woods. . . .
But there is no road through the woods!

RUDYARD KIPLING

THE LONELY TREE

Wilfrid Wilson Gibson is an Englishman whom Amy Lowell calls a "poet of harsh drama and rough tragedy." He was born in Northumberland and lives in Gloucestershire. He has published some twenty or more volumes of poetry and is one of the best known of modern writers. He has been a social worker in the slums of London, and served as a private in the British army during the Great War.

A twisted ash, a ragged fir,
A silver birch with leaves astir.

Men talk of forests broad and deep,
Where summer long the shadows sleep.

Though I love forests deep and wide,
The lone tree on the bare hillside,

The brave, wind-beaten, lonely tree
Is rooted in the heart of me.

A twisted ash, a ragged fir,
A silver birch with leaves astir.

WILFRID WILSON GIBSON

THE PINE AT TIMBER-LINE

Harriet Monroe was born in Chicago and educated at The Visitation Academy at Georgetown, D. C. She is the founder and editor of *Poetry, A Magazine of Verse.* She is the author of several volumes of poetry, and co-editor with Alice Corbin Henderson of an anthology called "The New Poetry."

In "The Pine at Timber-Line," words that show effort, resistance, a fight for life on the part of the lonely tree, are effectively contrasted with those in the smoothly flowing line which describes existence in

"The soft green valley of summer down below."

What has bent you,
Warped and twisted you,
Torn and crippled you?—
What has embittered you,
O lonely tree?

You search the rocks for a footing,
  dragging scrawny roots;
You bare your thin breast to the storms,
  and fling out wild arms behind you;
You throw back your witch-like head,
  with wisps of hair stringing the wind.

You fight with the snows,
You rail and shriek at the tempests.
Old before your time, you challenge the cold stars.

Be still, be satisfied!
Stand straight like your brothers in the valley,
The soft green valley of summer down below.

Why front the endless winter of the peak?
Why seize the lightning in your riven hands?
Why cut the driven wind and shriek aloud?

Why tarry here?

HARRIET MONROE

PRIAPUS

Keeper of Orchards

Hilda Doolittle (H. D.) is an American poet born at Bethlehem, Pennsylvania. She was educated at Bryn Mawr. She is the wife of Richard Aldington, the famous English Imagist. Untermeyer says: "H. D. is by all means the most important of her (the Imagist) group."

"Orchard" suggests a Greek garden. The details of its beauty are absolutely true to the facts and described in exact words. The writer almost shrinks from a loveliness that is too poignant, as all of us do when "we are so happy that it hurts."

> I saw the first pear
> As it fell.
> The honey-seeking, golden-banded,
> The yellow swarm
> Was not more fleet than I,
> (Spare us from loveliness!)
> And I fell prostrate,
> Crying,
> "Thou hast flayed us with thy blossoms;
> Spare us the beauty
> Of fruit-trees!"
>
> The honey-seeking
> Paused not,
> The air thundered their song,
> And I alone was prostrate.
>
> O rough-hewn
> God of the orchard,
> I bring thee an offering;
> Do thou, alone unbeautiful

(Son of the god),
Spare us from loveliness.

The fallen hazel-nuts,
Stripped late of their green sheaths,
The grapes, red-purple,
Their berries
Dripping with wine,
Pomegranates already broken,
And shrunken figs,
And quinces untouched,
I bring thee as offering.

H. D.

GOOD COMPANY

Karle Wilson Baker (née Wilson) was born in Little Rock,
Arkansas, and educated at the University of Chicago. Her early
poems appeared under the pen name of Charlotte Wilson. She
as published volumes of essays, fiction, and poetry, including
wo fairy books for children. She lives at Nacogdoches, Texas.

o-day I have grown taller from walking with the trees,
  The seven sister-poplars who go softly in a line;
nd I think my heart is whiter for its parley with a star
  That trembled out at nightfall and hung above the pine.

he call-note of a redbird from the cedars in the dusk
  Woke his happy mate within me to an answer free and fine;
nd a sudden angel beckoned from a column of blue smoke—
  *Lord, who am I that they should stoop—these holy folk of
    thine?*

                                        KARLE WILSON BAKER

THE SOUND OF THE TREES

Robert Frost's biography will be found in connection with "Birches."

"The Sound of the Trees" has more of the lyric or singing quality than has "Birches." The partial hush in the trees, then their renewed tossing and straining are in the rhythm. Only two lines are without one or more "s" sounds; some of these sharp, others very soft. The poet has a quaint fancy that under the spell of the trees his feet seem rooted to the ground and his head sways to his shoulder. But, unlike the trees, he will some day go, not talk about it.

I wonder about the trees.
Why do we wish to bear
Forever the noise of these
More than another noise
So close to our dwelling-place?
We suffer them by the day
Till we lose all measure of pace,
And fixity in our joys,
And acquire a listening air
They are that that talks of going
But never gets away;
And that talks no less for knowing,
As it grows wiser and older,
That now it means to stay.
My feet tug at the floor
And my head sways to my shoulder
Sometimes when I watch trees sway,
From the window or the door.
I shall set forth for somewhere,
I shall make the reckless choice
Some day when they are in voice

And tossing so as to scare
The white clouds over them on.
I shall have less to say,
But I shall be gone.

ROBERT FROST

THE CEDARS

Josephine Preston Peabody (Mrs. Marks) was born in New York City and educated in the Girls' Latin School of Boston and at Radcliffe. She taught two years at Wellesley. She died in 1922. Her play "The Piper" won the Stratford-on-Avon Prize and was produced in England and America. She was the author of nine other volumes of poetry.

All down the years the fragrance came,
The mingled fragrance, with a flame,
Of Cedars breathing in the sun,
The Cedar-trees of Lebanon.

O thirst of song in bitter air,
And hope, wing-hurt from iron care,
What balm of myrrh and honey, won
From far-off trees of Lebanon!

Not from these eyelids yet, have I
Ever beheld that early sky.
Why do they call me through the sun?—
Even the trees of Lebanon?

JOSEPHINE PRESTON PEABODY

POPLAR TREES ARE HAPPIEST

John Russell McCarthy has written for *Contemporary Verse*, *The Lyric West*, and other magazines. The personal facts of his life could not be ascertained.

The poplar tree has caught the fancy of many modern poets, as it formerly was dear to Cowper and Tennyson.

> Poplar trees are laughing trees,
> With lilting silver call,
> Willow trees droop weepingly
> And never laugh at all.
>
> Maple trees are gorgeous trees
> In crimson silks and gold;
> Pine trees are but sober trees,
> Aloof and very old.
>
> Black-oak trees walk sturdily,
> And live oaks eager run;
> The sycamores stand lazily
> Beneath the summer sun.
>
> But poplar trees are laughing trees
> Wherever they may grow—
> The poplar trees are happiest
> Of all the trees I know.
>
> JOHN RUSSELL McCARTHY

THE POPLAR

Richard Aldington was born in England and educated at London University. He is a leader of the Imagist group, of whom his wife, H. D. (Hilda Doolittle), is an American representative. He is a translator of classical poetry and author of several volumes of verse. He is assistant editor of *The Egoist*, a periodical.

Why do you always stand there shivering
Between the white stream and the road?

The people pass through the dust
On bicycles, in carts, in motor-cars;
The wagoners go by at dawn;
The lovers walk on the grass path at night.

Stir from your roots, walk, poplar!
You are more beautiful than they are.

I know that the white wind loves you,
Is always kissing you and turning up
The white lining of your green petticoat.
The sky darts through you like blue rain,
And the gray rain drips on your flanks
And loves you.
And I have seen the moon
Slip his silver penny into your pocket
As you straightened your hair;
And the white mist curling and hesitating
Like a bashful lover about your knees.

I know you, poplar;
I have watched you since I was ten.

But if you had a little real love,
A little strength,
You would leave your nonchalant idle lovers
And go walking down the white road
Behind the wagoners.

There are beautiful beeches
Down beyond the hill.
Will you always stand there shivering?

RICHARD ALDINGTON

THE MESSAGE

Dorothy Leonard was born in Connecticut. She was educated at Mt. Holyoke College and at Teachers College in New York City. She is a well-known contributor to leading periodicals.

The modern poet seldom preaches, but, as in "The Message," the inner meaning is clear. The verbs in this poem are especially good.

I saw the buds on the dogwood tree:
They made a message of May for me—
    Though winter is coming
    And cold skies lower,
    At the end of it all
    Is a day—is an hour—
    When oak leaves open
    Like butterflies' wings,
    And suddenly, somewhere,
    An oriole sings,
    And lilacs promise,
    And peonies prink,
    And dogwood petals
    Unfold in pink—
So winter may whistle for all of me,
O tight little buds on the dogwood tree!

DOROTHY LEONARD

SHADE

Theodosia Garrison (Mrs. Frederic J. Faulks) was born in Newark, New Jersey, and educated in private schools. She has published several volumes of poetry and is a frequent contributor to leading magazines.

The kindliest thing God ever made,
His hand of very healing laid
Upon a fevered world, is shade.

His glorious company of trees
Throw out their mantles, and on these
The dust-stained wanderer finds ease.

Green temples, closed against the beat
Of noontime's blinding glare and heat,
Open to any pilgrim's feet.

The white road blisters in the sun;
Now half the weary journey done,
Enter and rest, O weary one!

And feel the dew of dawn still wet
Beneath thy feet, and so forget
The burning highway's ache and fret.

This is God's hospitality,
And whoso rests beneath a tree
Hath cause to thank Him gratefully.

THEODOSIA GARRISON

YELLOW WARBLERS

Katharine Lee Bates was born at Falmouth, Massachusetts. She was educated at Wellesley, Middlebury, and Oberlin. She is the author of many books of prose and poetry, and was professor of English literature at Wellesley for many years.

Color words and colorific words—those that suggest color—make "Yellow Warblers" a dazzling bit of gold and blue against the background of the oak and the dawn. The tininess of the birds as suggested by "Live buds," "shining inches," "flakes of glee," is contrasted with the immensity of conception in the last stanza, where God broods over the universe, a "nest of stars."

The first faint dawn was flushing up the skies,
When, dreamland still bewildering mine eyes,
I looked out to the oak that, winter-long,—
A winter wild with war and woe and wrong,—
Beyond my casement had been void of song.

And lo! with golden buds the twigs were set,
Live buds that warbled like a rivulet
Beneath a veil of willows. Then I knew
Those tiny voices, clear as drops of dew,
Those flying daffodils that fleck the blue,

Those sparkling visitants from myrtle isles—
Wee pilgrims of the sun, that measured miles
Innumerable over land and sea
With wings of shining inches. Flakes of glee,
They filled that dark old oak with jubilee,

Foretelling in delicious roundelays
Their dainty courtships on the dipping sprays,
How they should fashion nests, mate helping mate,

Of milkweed flax and fern-down delicate,
To keep the sky-tinted eggs inviolate.

Listening to those blithe notes, I slipped once more
From lyric dawn through dreamland's open door,
And there was God, Eternal Life that sings
Eternal joy, brooding all mortal things,
A nest of stars, beneath untroubled wings.

KATHARINE LEE BATES

TO A PHŒBE BIRD

Witter Bynner, an American playwright, was born in Brooklyn and educated at Harvard. He is the author of many plays and volumes of poetry. With Arthur Davison Ficke he published "Spectra," writing under the name of Emanuel Morgan. During the World War he was a lecturer on English at the University of California. He has done much editorial work.

Under the eaves, out of the wet,
　　You nest within my reach;
You never sing for me and yet
　　You have a golden speech.

You sit and quirk a rapid tail,
　　Wrinkle a ragged crest,
Then pirouette from tree to rail
　　And vault from rail to nest.

And when in frequent, dainty fright
　　You grayly slip and fade,
And when at hand you re-alight
　　Demure and unafraid,

And when you bring your brood its fill
　　Of iridescent wings
And green legs dewy in your bill,
　　Your silence is what sings.

Not of a feather that enjoys
　　To prate or praise or preach,
O phœbe, with so little noise,
　　What eloquence you teach!

WITTER BYNNER

CANTICLE

William Griffith was born in Memphis, Missouri, and lives in New York. He is known as an editor and as the author of a number of books of verse.

> Devoutly worshiping the oak
> Wherein the barred owl stares,
> The little feathered forest folk
> Are praying sleepy prayers:
>
> Praying the summer to be long
> And drowsy to the end,
> And daily full of sun and song,
> That broken hopes may mend.
>
> Praying the golden age to stay
> Until the whippoorwill
> Appoints a windy moving day,
> And hurries from the hill.

WILLIAM GRIFFITH

Albion
College
Library

THE BLACK VULTURE

George Sterling was born in New York and educated at St. Charles College, Maryland. He lived in California and most of his poems are on Californian themes. He published many volumes of poetry.

"The Black Vulture" in its simplicity and imagery represents Mr. Sterling at his best. The poem suggests remoteness, detachment, and the great spaces typical of the West.

Aloof upon the day's immeasured dome,
    He holds unshared the silence of the sky.
    Far down, his bleak, relentless eyes descry
The eagle's empire and the falcon's home—
Far down, the galleons of sunset roam;
    His hazards on the sea of morning lie;
    Serene, he hears the broken tempest sigh
Where cold sierras gleam like scattered foam.

And least of all he holds the human swarm—
    Unwitting now that envious men prepare
    To make their dream and its fulfilment one,
When, poised above the caldrons of the storm,
    Their hearts, contemptuous of death, shall dare
    His roads between the thunder and the sun.

                        GEORGE STERLING

WHEN THE FROST IS ON THE PUNKIN

James Whitcomb Riley was born in Greenfield, Indiana, the son of a prosperous lawyer. He studied law, journeyed about with a company of strolling players, and worked on a newspaper before he finally settled down to his life-work—recording in poetry the life of the Middle West. He lived most of his life in Indianapolis, and died there at his home in Lockerbie Street in 1916. The Riley Hospital, the largest in the world for the cure of crippled children, is maintained in Indianapolis in his memory.

Riley is often a realist, as in this poem, "When the Frost Is on the Punkin." This farm scene is typical of that region of which Indiana is a part. The well-filled barns, the animated barnyards, the cellar floor bright with heaped apples, are not invented signs of plenty. And he is faithful in word and image to the sights and sounds of the out-of-doors. See, for instance, the colors in the corn-fields and listen to the wind blowing through them:

"The husky, rusty russel of the tossels of the corn,
    And the raspin' of the tangled leaves as golden as the morn."

When the frost is on the punkin and the fodder's in the shock,
And you hear the kyouck and gobble of the struttin' turkey-
                cock,
And the clackin' of the guineys, and the cluckin' of the hens,
And the rooster's hallylooer as he tiptoes on the fence;
O, it's then the time a feller is a-feelin' at his best,
With the risin' sun to greet him from a night of peaceful rest,
As he leaves the house, bareheaded, and goes out to feed the
                stock,
When the frost is on the punkin and the fodder's in the shock.

They's something kind o' harty-like about the atmusfere
When the heat of summer's over and the coolin' fall is here—
Of course we miss the flowers, and the blossoms on the trees,

And the mumble of the hummin'-birds and buzzin' of the
    bees;
But the air's so appetizin'; and the landscape through the
    haze
Of a crisp and sunny morning of the airly autumn days
Is a pictur' that no painter has the colorin' to mock—
When the frost is on the punkin and the fodder's in the shock.

The husky, rusty russel of the tossels of the corn,
And the raspin' of the tangled leaves as golden as the morn;
The stubble in the furries—kind o' lonesome-like, but still
A-preachin' sermuns to us of the barns they growed to fill;
The strawstack in the medder, and the reaper in the shed;
The hosses in theyr stalls below—the clover overhead!—
O, it sets my hart a-clickin' like the tickin' of a clock,
When the frost is on the punkin and the fodder's in the shock.

Then your apples all is gethered, and the ones a feller keeps
Is poured around the cellar-floor in red and yaller heaps;
And your cider-makin's over. and your wimmern-folks is
    through
With theyr mince and apple-butter, and theyr souse and
    sausage too! . . .
I don't know how to tell it—but if such a thing could be
As the angels wantin' boardin', and they'd call around on
    me—
I'd want to 'commodate 'em—all the whole-indurin' flock—
When the frost is on the punkin and the fodder's in the shock.

                              JAMES WHITCOMB RILEY

A BALLADE–CATALOGUE OF LOVELY THINGS

Richard Le Gallienne was born in Liverpool, England. He was educated at Liverpool College. He is a frequent contributor to magazines and writes also essays and criticisms. He is the author of some fifty volumes of prose and poetry. He lives in New York City.

"A Ballade-Catalogue of Lovely Things" is modelled after a French form of the fourteenth and fifteenth centuries. It requires three stanzas and an envoi, and a refrain that must be repeated at the close of each stanza and at the close of the envoi. Only three or four rhymes are permitted, and these must be repeated exactly in each division. The envoi completes the poem by binding together the rest and emphasizing the message. In this poem the writer has successfully met these conditions and has also reproduced the courtly spirit of mediæval days, but the images are truly American.

I would make a list against the evil days
  Of lovely things to hold in memory:
First, I would set down my lady's lovely face,
  For earth has no such lovely thing as she;
  And next I add, to bear her company,
The great-eyed virgin star that morning brings;
  Then the wild rose upon its little tree—
So runs my catalogue of lovely things.

The enchanted dogwood, with its ivory trays,
  The water-lily in its sanctuary
Of reeded pools, and dew-drenched lilac sprays,
  For these, of all fair flowers, the fairest be;
  Next write I down the great name of the sea,
Lonely in greatness as the names of kings;
  Then the young moon that hath us all in fee—
So runs my catalogue of lovely things.

Imperial sunsets that in crimson blaze
  Along the hills, and, fairer still to me,
The fireflies dancing in a netted maze
  Woven of twilight and tranquillity;
  Shakespeare and Virgil, their high poesy;
Then a great ship, splendid with snowy wings,
  Voyaging on into eternity—
So runs my catalogue of lovely things.

ENVOI

Prince, not the gold bars of thy treasury,
  Not all thy jewelled sceptres, crowns and rings,
Are worth the honeycomb of the wild bee—
  So runs my catalogue of lovely things.

RICHARD LE GALLIENNE

THE HARP OF THE WIND

Frances Shaw was born in Chicago, where she still lives. She was educated at the Dearborn Seminary and at Farmington, Connecticut. She has written several volumes of verse, some of which are child poems. Her methods are those of the Imagists.

"The Harp of the Wind" is a delicate and sustained metaphor with a well-defined pattern. The third stanza in its rhythmic plan suggests the harp-strings on which the wind plays the "song of life."

My house stands high—
Where the harp of the wind
Plays all day,
Plays all night;
And the city light
Is far away.

Where hangs the harp that the winds play?—
High in the air—
Over the sea?

The long straight streets of the far-away town,
Where the lines of light go sweeping down,
Are the strings of its minstrelsy.

And the harp of the wind
Gives to the wind
A song of the city's tears;
Thin and faint, the cry of a child,
Plaint of the soul unreconciled,
A song of the passing years.

FRANCES SHAW

THE RUNNER IN THE SKIES

James Oppenheim was born at St. Paul, Minnesota. He has
lived in New York City since he was two years old. He was
educated in the New York public schools and studied two years
in Columbia University. For three years he did settlement work.
Since then he has devoted himself to poetry, of which he has
produced a number of volumes.

"The Runner in the Skies" shows Mr. Oppenheim at his best.
Like David of old, he contemplates in wonder the mysteries of
the heavens.

Who is the runner in the skies,

With her blowing scarf of stars,

And our earth and sun hovering like bees about her blossom-
ing heart!

Her feet are on the winds where space is deep;

Her eyes are nebulous and veiled;

She hurries through the night to a far lover.

JAMES OPPENHEIM

FOG

Carl Sandburg was born at Galesburg, Illinois. In 1898 he served in the war with Spain. On his return he entered Lombard College in Galesburg. He is now an editorial writer on the Chicago *Daily News* and one of the best-known poets of America.

"Fog" is a much-liked bit of symbolism. "Words are magic," said Whitman, and "Fog" illustrates his declaration. Silence, stealth, and mysterious uncertainty of purpose are characteristic of both cat and fog.

> The fog comes
> on little cat feet.
>
> It sits looking
> over harbor and city
> on silent haunches
> and then moves on.

CARL SANDBURG

GHOSTS

Marguerite Wilkinson's biography has been given in connection with "A Chant Out-of-Doors."

You say you saw a ghost, in the house, at night,
Standing stiff and chilly in evanescent silver,
In your room, near the bed where your grandfather died.
But I saw ghosts, hundreds of them, dancing,
Out-of-doors, by day, in a dazzle of sunlight,
Climbing through the air of a clearing near the river,
Flying dizzily there in a brief puff of the breeze,
Yes, hundreds of ghosts, where a little while ago
Died hundreds of the purple blooms of the thistle.

MARGUERITE WILKINSON

OLD MANUSCRIPT

Alfred Kreymborg lives in New York City, where he was born. He has been a teacher of chess-playing and a bookkeeper. He is devoted to music. He has published several volumes of his own verse, and anthologies of the verse of the group called "Others."

> The sky
> is that beautiful old parchment
> in which the sun
> and the moon
> keep their diary.
> To read it all,
> one must be a linguist
> more learned than Father Wisdom;
> and a visionary
> more clairvoyant than Mother Dream.
> But to feel it,
> one must be an apostle:
> one who is more than intimate
> in having been, always,
> the only confidant—
> like the earth
> or the sea.

ALFRED KREYMBORG

MONOTONE

For the biographical sketch of Carl Sandburg, see "Fog."
"Monotone" has the speaking rather than the lyric rhythm, and its cadences are long and flowing. There is the sonnet feeling although not the sonnet form. The beauty of summary is illustrated in the last stanza.

The monotone of the rain is beautiful,
And the long sudden rise and the slow relapse
Of the long multitudinous rain

The sun on the hills is beautiful,
Or a captured sunset, sea-flung,
Bannered with fire and gold.

A face I know is beautiful—
With fire and gold of sky and sea,
And the peace of the long warm rain.

CARL SANDBURG

THE OLD PLOUGH–HORSE

Mahlon Leonard Fisher was born in Williamsport, Pennsylvania. He was educated in the high school and by private instruction. He studied and practised architecture. In 1917 he founded the magazine called *The Sonnet*.

In Mr. Fisher's hands the sonnet is a wonderful expression of mood. Here, in "The Old Plough-Horse," the movement is slow and the atmosphere is "dream-drawn and a-drowse," as befits the theme.

Worn-out and useless, lone, he stands and dreams,
   Day after day, the long sweet summer through:
   The last turf-ridge upturned, what is to do
Save watch the crow-hordes, or a hawk that screams
High o'er his master's dooryard, till it seems
   The world was made a place for dreaming in?
   Around him, daisy-wheels ecstatic spin,
And cattle splash, knee-deep, through cooling streams;
But he, inert, thought-wrapt, oblivious, drifts,
   Dream-drawn, a-drowse, towards other fields than these,
   Where first he felt the Spring's quick kiss, and seas
Of green about him swam. . . . His bent head lifts . . .
   Like some sweet message caught from far-off lands,
   He hears his mother whinny, where he stands!

MAHLON LEONARD FISHER

SILVER

Walter de la Mare was born at Charlton in Kent, England.
He was educated in London at St. Paul's Cathedral Choir School.
He was employed for some years in the English offices of the
Standard Oil Company of America.   Since 1902 he has published
many volumes of verse.

"Silver" is another proof that "words are magic."   Liquids
and vowels in such words as "moon," "shoon," "silver," "sleep,"
"moveless," "gleam," slip into cool, flowing rhythms.   Every
detail of the picture is perfect and can be verified by all who
have seen the witchery of moonlight.

> Slowly, silently, now the moon
> Walks the night in her silver shoon;
> This way, and that, she peers and sees
> Silver fruit upon silver trees;
> One by one the casements catch
> Her beams beneath the silvery thatch;
> Couched in his kennel, like a log,
> With paws of silver sleeps the dog;
> From their shadowy cote the white breasts peep
> Of doves in a silver-feathered sleep;
> A harvest mouse goes scampering by,
> With silver claws, and a silver eye;
> And moveless fish in the water gleam,
> By silver reeds in a silver stream.

                                    WALTER DE LA MARE

THE FOUNTAIN

For the biographical sketch of Sara Teasdale, see "Barter."

Fountain, fountain, what do you say,
Singing at night alone?
"It is enough to rise and fall
Here in my basin of stone."

But are you content as you seem to be
So near the freedom and rush of the sea?
"I have listened all night to its laboring sound,
It heaves and sags, as the moon runs round:
Ocean and fountain, shadow and tree,
Nothing escapes, nothing is free."

                              SARA TEASDALE

MAY IS BUILDING HER HOUSE

For the biographical sketch of Richard Le Gallienne, see "A
Ballade-Catalogue of Lovely Things."

May is building her house. With apple blooms
She is roofing over the glimmering rooms;
   Of the oak and the beech hath she builded its beams,
And, spinning all day at her secret looms,
     With arras of leaves each wind-swayed wall
     She pictureth over, and peopleth it all
    With echoes and dreams,
    And singing of streams.

May is building her house of petal and blade;
Of the roots of the oak is the flooring made,
   With a carpet of mosses and lichen and clover
   Each small miracle over and over,
And tender, travelling green things strayed

Her windows, the morning and evening star,
And her rustling doorways, ever ajar
   With the coming and going
   Of fair things blowing,
The thresholds of the four winds are.

May is building her house. From the dust of things
She is making the songs and the flowers and the wings;
   From October's tossed and trodden gold
   She is making the young year out of the old;
    Yea: out of the winter's flying sleet

She is making all the summer sweet,
And the brown leaves spurned of November's feet
She is changing back again to spring's.

RICHARD LE GALLIENNE

SPRING

John Gould Fletcher was born in Little Rock, Arkansas. He was educated at Phillips Academy, Andover, and at Harvard, and by sojourns in western America and in Italy. He lives in London, where he writes largely of America. He and H. D. and Amy Lowell are the three foremost American Imagists.

"Spring" gravely and beautifully describes the twelve creative hours. The poem hints of the Easter miracle toward which all hearts yearn.

At the first hour, it was as if one said, "Arise."
At the second hour, it was as if one said, "Go forth."
And the winter constellations that are like patient ox-eyes
Sank below the white horizon at the north.

At the third hour, it was as if one said, "I thirst";
At the fourth hour, all the earth was still:
Then the clouds suddenly swung over, stooped, and burst;
And the rain flooded valley, plain, and hill.

At the fifth hour, darkness took the throne;
At the sixth hour, the earth shook and the wind cried;
At the seventh hour, the hidden seed was sown,
At the eighth hour, it gave up the ghost and died.

At the ninth hour, they sealed up the tomb;
And the earth was then silent for the space of three hours.
But at the twelfth hour, a single lily from the gloom
Shot forth, and was followed by a whole host of flowers.

JOHN GOULD FLETCHER

A DAY

Emily Dickinson was born in Amherst, Massachusetts, December 10, 1830, and died May 15, 1886, in the house in which she was born and which she rarely left. Some of her poems were first brought together and published in 1890. Two successive volumes brought other poems to the attention of the world. In all, there were more than five hundred. They are works of originality rather than of tradition. Their exactness and newness of epithet and their clearness of imagery are in line with the later gospel of the Imagists. Emily Dickinson's life was a life of inner, rather than outer, event. Louis Untermeyer says: "Emily Dickinson's firm delicacy was the result of emotion discovered, analyzed, and restrained."

I'll tell you how the sun rose,—
A ribbon at a time,
The steeples swam in amethyst,
The news like squirrels ran.

The hills untied their bonnets,
The bobolinks begun.
Then I said softly to myself,
"That must have been the sun."

But how he set, I know not.
There seemed a purple stile
Which little yellow boys and girls
Were climbing all the while,

Till when they reached the other side,
A dominie in gray
Put gently up the evening bars,
And led the flock away.

EMILY DICKINSON

THE CITY DWELLER

Bernice Kenyon (Mrs. T. Walter Gilkyson) was born in New-ton, Massachusetts. She is a graduate of Wellesley. She was the winner of the Masefield Poetry Prize at Wellesley in 1920, the year of her graduation. She has published a volume of poetry.

"The City Dweller" speaks for all who yearn for Nature in the open, and resort to the make-believe which finds in blown smoke a reminder of birds and in the motion of men the sound of the sea.

These things I cannot forget: far snow in the night,
    The shadows of hills, and the leaping beauty of flame,
Wind-scattered leaves, and the patterns of birds in flight,
    And the changing thunderous sea that is never the same.

Oh, high are the city walls, and the houses tall,
    And only the sky remains of beautiful things,
And there never is time to search the sky at all,
    Lest there pass above me the changing pattern of wings.

But youth, clear youth that breathes in my breath to-day,
    Chants in my blood that ancient beauty is young;
And sees far snow in the lamp-lit snow of my way,
    And shadows of hills where the long wall-shadows are flung,

And flaming fire is lit by the million lights,
    And blown smoke gathers as birds, or as leaves wind-free;
And oh, if your eyes are closed in the clamorous nights,
    The motion of men resounds like the thundering sea!

BERNICE KENYON

REAL PROPERTY

Harold Monro was born in Brussels. He founded the Poetry
Bookshop in London in 1912. This bookshop has been the meeting-place of the younger poets of the day, and his successive
magazines, *Poetry and the Drama* and *The Chapbook*, have contained many of their poems. He has published several volumes
of his own poems.

"Real Property" is not only good poetry but good advice as
well. It shows how one may appropriate wheat-fields and other
lovely things without wronging the man in whose name the
property is recorded. And the possession is permanent:

> "You only need to close your eyes
> And go within your secret mind,
> And you'll be into paradise."

Tell me about that harvest-field.
Oh! Fifty acres of living bread.
The color has painted itself in my heart.
The form is patterned in my head.

So now I take it everywhere;
See it whenever I look round;
Hear it growing through every sound,
Know exactly the sound it makes—
Remembering, as one must all day,
Under the pavement the live earth aches.

Trees are at the farther end,
Limes all full of the mumbling bee;
So there must be a harvest-field
Whenever one thinks of a linden tree.

A hedge is about it, very tall,
Hazy and cool, and breathing sweet.

Round paradise is such a wall
And all the day, in such a way,
In paradise the wild birds call.

You only need to close your eyes
And go within your secret mind,
And you'll be into paradise:
I've learnt quite easily to find
Some linden trees and drowsy bees,
A tall sweet hedge with the corn behind.

I will not have that harvest mown;
I'll keep the corn and leave the bread.
I've bought that field; it's now my own:
I've fifty acres in my head.
I take it as a dream to bed.
I carry it about all day. . . .

Sometimes when I have found a friend
I give a blade of corn away.

HAROLD MONRO

NATURE'S FRIEND

William H. Davies was born in Wales at Newport. His adventurous spirit took him across the Atlantic several times and sent him tramping over the world. He had very little money, a fact that troubled him not at all. While he was trying to board a train in Canada, he lost a foot. His only education was from travel and his sympathy with Nature. Having written a few lyrics, he had them published, and sent a copy to Bernard Shaw with the request that the book be returned or paid for. Bernard Shaw recognized the merit of the poems and helped the author to a hearing by the public.

Like other poets of to-day, Davies does not patronize Nature. Rather is he Nature's friend. His poetry is so unaffected, so cheerful, that we feel like slipping out-of-doors and saying with him:

> "Good morning, Life—and all
>   Things glad and beautiful."

Say what you like,
   All things love me!
I pick no flowers—
   That wins the Bee.

The Summer's Moths
   Think my hand one—
To touch their wings—
   With Wind and Sun.

The garden Mouse
   Comes near to play;
Indeed, he turns
   His eyes away.

The Wren knows well
   I rob no nest;

When I look in,
  She still will rest.

The hedge stops Cows,
  Or they would come
After my voice
  Right to my home.

The Horse can tell
  Straight from my lip,
My hand could not
  Hold any whip.

Say what you like,
  All things love me!
Horse, Cow, and Mouse,
  Bird, Moth, and Bee.

WILLIAM H. DAVIES

WAR, PATRIOTISM, AND PEACE

THE FIELDS

For the biographical sketch of Witter Bynner, see "To a Phœbe-Bird."

Though wisdom underfoot
Dies in the bloody fields,
Slowly the endless root
Gathers again and yields.

In fields where hate has hurled
Its force, where folly rots,
Wisdom shall be uncurled
Small as forget-me-nots.

WITTER BYNNER

THE TOY BAND

A Song of the Great Retreat

Sir Henry Newbolt was born in England. He was educated at Oxford and became a barrister at Lincoln's Inn. He is widely known for his ballads of the sea and for the stirring measure that beats through all his poems.

"The Toy Band" tells how soldiers in the World War, dead for sleep, are roused to marching spirit by a toy fife and a child's drum. The poem resounds with marching feet, the "wheedle" of the fife, and the "rubadub" of the drum.

Dreary lay the long road, dreary lay the town,
    Lights out and never a glint of moon:
Weary lay the stragglers, half a thousand down,
    Sad sighed the weary big Dragoon.
"Oh! if I'd a drum here to make them take the road again,
    Oh! if I'd a fife to wheedle, Come, boys, come!
You that mean to fight it out, wake and take your load again,
    Fall in! Fall in! Follow the fife and drum!

"Hey, but here's a toy shop, here's a drum for me,
    Penny whistles too to play the tune!
Half a thousand dead men soon shall hear and see
    We're a band!" said the weary big Dragoon.
"Rubadub! Rubadub! Wake and take the road again,
    Wheedle-deedle-deedle-dee, Come, boys, come,
You that mean to fight it out, wake and take your load again,
    Fall in! Fall in! Follow the fife and drum!"

Cheerly goes the dark road, cheerly goes the night,
    Cheerly goes the blood to keep the beat:
Half a thousand dead men marching on to fight
    With a little penny drum to lift their feet.

Rubadub! Rubadub! Wake and take the road again,
  Wheedle-deedle-deedle-dee, Come, boys, come!
You that mean to fight it out, wake and take your load again,
  Fall in! Fall in! Follow the fife and drum!

As long as there's an Englishman to ask a tale of me,
  As long as I can tell the tale aright,
We'll not forget the penny whistle's Wheedle-deedle-dee
  And the big Dragoon a-beating down the night,
Rubadub! Rubadub! Wake and take the road again,
  Wheedle-deedle-deedle-dee, Come, boys, come!
You that mean to fight it out, wake and take your load again,
  Fall in! Fall in! Follow the fife and drum!

SIR HENRY NEWBOLT

I HAVE A RENDEZVOUS WITH DEATH

Alan Seeger was born in New York City and educated at Harvard. At the very beginning of the World War he joined the Foreign Legion in France, and there gave his young life in battle, July 4, 1916. His "Poems" were published the same year.

I have a rendezvous with Death
At some disputed barricade,
When Spring comes round with rustling shade
And apple-blossoms fill the air—
I have a rendezvous with Death
When Spring brings back blue days and fair.

It may be he shall take my hand
And lead me into his dark land
And close my eyes and quench my breath—
It may be I shall pass him still.
I have a rendezvous with Death
On some scarred slope of battered hill,
When Spring comes round again this year
And the first meadow-flowers appear.

God knows 'twere better to be deep
Pillowed in silk and scented down,
Where Love throbs out in blissful sleep,
Pulse nigh to pulse, and breath to breath,
Where hushed awakenings are dear. . . .
But I've a rendezvous with Death
At midnight in some flaming town,
When Spring trips north again this year,
And I to my pledged word am true,
I shall not fail that rendezvous.

ALAN SEEGER

IN FLANDERS FIELDS

John McCrae was a Canadian born in Scotland. He received his A.B. and his M.D. degrees from the University of Toronto, and took special work at Johns Hopkins. He was a lieutenant-colonel in charge of the Medical Division of the McGill Canadian General Hospital in France in the World War. He died of pneumonia in 1918.

"In Flanders Fields" records contrasts—death and roaring guns, singing larks and scarlet poppy-fields—which were realities to Dr. McCrae, who was in active service in Flanders during the World War. The poem is a perfect example of that difficult French form called the rondeau. It has thirteen lines on two lines of unrhyming refrain. The refrain, "In Flanders fields," is a repetition of the first three words of the poem and is unrhymed. The last stanza constitutes the postscript (l'envoi), which urges the poem's message.

The insistence upon poppies suggests their sleep-giving power.

> In Flanders fields the poppies blow
> Between the crosses, row on row,
>   That mark our place; and in the sky
>   The larks, still bravely singing, fly
> Scarce heard amid the guns below.
>
> We are the Dead. Short days ago
> We lived, felt dawn, saw sunset glow,
>   Loved and were loved, and now we lie
>   In Flanders fields.
>
> Take up our quarrel with the foe:
> To you from failing hands we throw
>   The torch; be yours to hold it high.
>   If ye break faith with us who die
> We shall not sleep, though poppies grow
>   In Flanders fields.
>   JOHN McCRAE

THE SPIRES OF OXFORD

As Seen from the Train

Winifred M. Letts was born in Ireland. She has written many poems about the Irish peasant, also novels, children's books, and a volume of war poems. During the World War she served as a nurse in base hospitals.

In "The Spires of Oxford," a much-loved poem, the contrast between "The hoary Colleges" and "careless boys at play" makes a very tender appeal. Youth has always been foremost in giving its life "For country and for God." We remember that the great English universities time and again have given the best of their young men to fight the wars of England.

I saw the spires of Oxford
As I was passing by,
The gray spires of Oxford
Against a pearl-gray sky.
My heart was with the Oxford men
Who went abroad to die.

The years go fast in Oxford,
The golden years and gay,
The hoary Colleges look down
On careless boys at play.
But when the bugles sounded war,
They put their games away.

They left the peaceful river,
The cricket-field, the quad,
The shaven lawns of Oxford
To seek a bloody sod—
They gave their merry youth away
For country and for God.

God rest you, happy gentlemen,
Who laid your good lives down,
Who took the khaki and the gun
Instead of cap and gown.
God bring you to a fairer place
Than even Oxford town.

WINIFRED M. LETTS

SOLDIER

Rupert Brooke was born at Rugby, England. He was educated at Rugby, Cambridge, and Munich. Edward Thomas
called him "a golden young Apollo"; and Louis Untermeyer
quotes another friend as saying: "To look at, he was a part of
the youth of the world." His education was completed by travel
in Europe, the United States, Canada, Samoa, and Tahiti. He
joined the British army on the outbreak of the Great War and
died on his way to the Dardanelles, April 23, 1915.

If I should die, think only this of me:
    That there's some corner of a foreign field
That is forever England. There shall be
    In that rich earth a richer dust concealed;
A dust whom England bore, shaped, made aware,
    Gave, once, her flowers to love, her ways to roam,
A body of England's, breathing English air,
    Washed by the rivers, blest by suns of home.
And think, this heart, all evil shed away,
    A pulse in the eternal mind, no less
      Gives somewhere back the thoughts by England given
Her sights and sounds; dreams happy as her day;
    And laughter, learnt of friends; and gentleness,
      In hearts at peace, under an English heaven.

                      RUPERT BROOKE

THE HEART OF THE BUGLE

Meredith Nicholson was born at Crawfordsville, Indiana. He was educated at Wabash College, Crawfordsville, and at Butler College, Indianapolis. He is a poet and a novelist of distinction. He lives in Indianapolis.

When, at Old Point Comfort in Virginia, Mr. Nicholson heard the bugle blowing at Fortress Monroe, he wrote the poem, "The Heart of the Bugle." It is a tribute to the heroism of his father, Edward Willis Nicholson, who, in the Civil War, was with General Lew Wallace of the Eleventh Indiana Regiment, and later was captain of the Twenty-second Indiana Battery.

I have heard the bugle blown
Where the southern seas make moan;
And have followed east and west
At its trumpeted behest;
By the mighty mountains' marge
I have heard it sing the charge,
Till old battles in my blood
Were a mighty tide at flood—
                    O bugle!

I have seen the bugler stand
With the trumpet in his hand,
When the winter's dawn light gray
Brought again reluctant day,
Very silent, very lone,
With the whole world for his own,
Till he woke it with a note
From the brazen trumpet's throat—
                    O bugle!

Then I saw old battles fade
Far across the dim parade,

And a thousand knights went by
Like a moving tapestry;
Old crusaders riding fast
Down dark vistas of the past,
Worn and broken in their mail
While the bugle sang them hail—
              O bugle!

As within the fort's grim bound
Swift the bugler made his round,
Dawn and youth were in the call
That he sent from wall to wall!
I saw Troy and Marathon
In the faint light of the dawn;
Battles old and battles new—
Agincourt and Waterloo—
              O bugle!

Now my blood more swiftly beats
Victories and brave defeats;—
Shiloh passes and I see
Swing in place a battery
With plunging horses seared and scourged,
By an undaunted leader urged,
And in that smoke-hung, fire-swept place
I see—through tears—my father's face—
              O bugle!

MEREDITH NICHOLSON

ON THE PORCH

For the biographical sketch of Harriet Monroe, see "The Pine at Timber-Line."

In "On the Porch" the rain suggests that other scene where cannons roar and aeroplane motors throb. From this uproar and strain the reader is relieved by the beautiful "return" of the last six lines.

As I lie roofed in, screened in,
From the pattering rain,
The summer rain—
As I lie
Snug and dry,
And hear the birds complain:

Oh, billow on billow,
Oh, roar on roar,
Over me wash
The seas of war.
Over me—down—down—
Lunges and plunges
The huge gun with its one blind eye,
The armored train,
And, swooping out of the sky,
The aeroplane.

Down—down—
The army proudly swinging
Under gay flags,
The glorious dead heaped up like rags,
A church with bronze bells ringing,
A city all towers,
Gardens of lovers and flowers,

The round world swinging
In the light of the sun:
All broken, undone,
All down—under
Black surges of thunder . . .

Oh, billow on billow,
Oh, roar on roar,
Over me wash
The seas of war . . .

As I lie roofed in, screened in,
From the pattering rain,
The summer rain—
As I lie
Snug and dry,
And hear the birds complain.

HARRIET MONROE

LINCOLN, THE MAN OF THE PEOPLE

Edwin Markham is poet, educator, and lecturer. He was born in Oregon and spent his boyhood years on a ranch in California. He was educated at San Jose Normal School. He was made famous in 1899 by "The Man with the Hoe." Since 1901 he has made his home on Staten Island, New York.

In "Lincoln" the imagery which finds in the man "the smack and tang of elemental things" is worked out in beautiful detail. Lincoln, the product of earth but Thinker and Leader, is in sharp contrast with the low-browed "Man with the Hoe," who too is of the earth but has never been released from the strangle-hold of Things.

When the Norn Mother saw the Whirlwind Hour
Greatening and darkening as it hurried on,
She left the Heaven of Heroes and came down
To make a man to meet the mortal need.
She took the tried clay of the common road
Clay warm yet with the genial heat of Earth,
Dashed through it all a strain of prophecy;
Tempered the heap with thrill of human tears;
Then mixed a laughter with the serious stuff.
Into the shape she breathed a flame to light
That tender, tragic, ever-changing face,
And laid on him a sense of the Mystic Powers,
Moving—all hushed—behind the mortal veil.
Here was a man to hold against the world,
A man to match the mountains and the sea.

The color of the ground was in him, the red earth,
The smack and tang of elemental things:
The rectitude and patience of the cliff;
The good-will of the rain that loves all leaves;

The friendly welcome of the wayside well;
The courage of the bird that dares the sea;
The gladness of the wind that shakes the corn;
The pity of the snow that hides all scars;
The secrecy of streams that make their way
Under the mountain to the rifted rock;
The tolerance and equity of light
That gives as freely to the shrinking flower
As to the great oak flaring to the wind—
To the grave's low hill as to the Matterhorn
That shoulders out the sky. Sprung from the West
He drank the valorous youth of a new world.
The strength of virgin forests braced his mind;
The hush of spacious prairies stilled his soul.
His words were oaks in acorns; and his thoughts
Were roots that firmly gripped the granite truth.

Up from the log cabin to the Capitol,
One fire was on his spirit, one resolve—
To send the keen axe to the root of wrong,
Clearing a free way for the feet of God,
The eyes of conscience testing every stroke,
To make his deed the measure of a man.
He built the rail-pile as he built the State,
Pouring his splendid strength through every blow.
The grip that swung the axe in Illinois
Was on the pen that set a people free.
So came the Captain with the mighty heart;
And when the judgment thunders split the house,
Wrenching the rafters from their ancient rest,
He held the ridgepole up, and spiked again
The rafters of the Home. He held his place—
Held the long purpose like a growing tree—

Held on through blame and faltered not at praise.
And when he fell in whirlwind, he went down
As when a lordly cedar, green with boughs,
Goes down with a great shout upon the hills,
And leaves a lonesome place against the sky.

EDWIN MARKHAM

FLEURETTE

Robert W. Service is a Canadian, born in England and educated in Scotland. He spent eight years in the Yukon, and
drove a Red Cross ambulance during the World War. His newspaper verse is syndicated throughout the country. He has published several volumes of verse.

(*The Wounded Canadian Speaks*)
1916

My leg? It's off at the knee.
Do I miss it? Well, some. You see
I've had it since I was born;
And lately a devilish corn.
(I rather chuckle with glee
To think how I've fooled that corn.)

But I'll hobble around all right.
It isn't that, it's my face.
Oh, I know I'm a hideous sight,
Hardly a thing in place.
Sort of gargoyle, you'd say.
Nurse won't give me a glass,
But I see the folks as they pass
Shudder and turn away;
Turn away in distress . . .
Mirror enough, I guess.
I'm gay! You bet I *am* gay;
But I wasn't a while ago.
If you'd seen me even to-day,
The darndest picture of woe,
With this Caliban mug of mine,
So ravaged and raw and red,

Turned to the wall—in fine
Wishing that I was dead . . .
What has happened since then,
Since I lay with my face to the wall,
The most despairing of men?
Listen! I'll tell you all.

That *poilu** across the way,
With the shrapnel wound on his head,
Has a sister; she came to-day
To sit a while by his bed.
All morning I heard him fret:
"Oh, when will she come, Fleurette?"

Then, sudden, a joyous cry;
The tripping of little feet;
The softest, tenderest sigh;
A voice so fresh and sweet;
Clear as a silver bell,
Fresh as the morning dews:
"*C'est toi, c'est toi, Marcel!
Mon frère, comme je suis heureuse!*†

So over the blanket's rim
I raised my terrible face,
And I saw—how I envied him!
A girl of such delicate grace;
Sixteen, all laughter and love;
As gay as a linnet, and yet
As tenderly sweet as a dove;
Half woman, half child—Fleurette.

---

* *Poilu*, a French soldier.
† *C'est toi*, etc.: "It is you, Marcel! My brother, how happy I am!"

Then I turned to the wall again.
(I was awfully blue, you see),
And I thought with a bitter pain:
"Such visions are not for me."
So there like a log I lay,
All hidden, I thought, from view,
When sudden I heard her say:
"Ah! Who is that *malheureux?*" *

Then briefly I heard him tell
(However he came to know)
How I'd smothered a bomb that fell
Into the trench, and so
None of my men were hit,
Though it busted me up a bit.

Well, I didn't quiver an eye,
And he chattered and there she sat;
And I fancied I heard her sigh—
But I wouldn't just swear to that.
And maybe she wasn't so bright,
Though she talked in a merry strain,
And I closed my eyes ever so tight,
Yet I saw her ever so plain:
Her dear little tilted nose,
Her delicate, dimpled chin,
Her mouth like a budding rose,
And the glistening pearls within;
Her eyes like the violet:
Such a rare little queen—Fleurette.

* *Malheureux*, unhappy one.

And at last when she rose to go
The light was a little dim,
And I ventured to peep, and so
I saw her graceful and slim,
And she kissed him and kissed him, and oh
How I envied and envied him!

So when she was gone I said
In rather a dreary voice
To him of the opposite bed:
"Ah, friend, how you must rejoice!
But me, I'm a thing of dread.
For me nevermore the bliss,
The thrill of a woman's kiss."

Then I stopped, for lo! she was there,
And a great light shone in her eyes.
And me! I could only stare,
I was taken so by surprise,
When gently she bent her head:
"May I kiss you, sergeant?" she said.
Then she kissed my burning lips,
With her mouth like a scented flower,
And I thrilled to the finger-tips,
And I hadn't even the power
To say: "God bless you, dear!"
And I felt such a precious tear
Fall on my withered cheek,
And, darn it, I couldn't speak.

And so she went sadly away,
And I know that my eyes were wet.
Ah, not to my dying day

Will I forget, forget!
Can you wonder now I am gay?
God bless her, that little Fleurette!

ROBERT W. SERVICE

REFUGEES

Belgium—1914

For the biographical sketch of Grace Hazard Conkling, see "After Sunset."

In "Refugees" the poplars give local color to the poem, for the roads of France and Belgium are often outlined by these trees, standing tall and protecting, with little foliage except a cluster at the top. The movement of the refugees is felt throughout the poem. Thus in the first stanza we see "the poplars cross the moon."

"Mother, the poplars cross the moon;
  The road runs on, so white and far,
We shall not reach the city soon:
  Oh, tell me where we are!"

"Have patience, patience, little son,
  And we shall find the way again:
(God show me the untravelled one!
  God give me rest from men!)"

"Mother, you did not tell me why
  You hurried so to come away.
I saw big soldiers riding by;
  I should have liked to stay."

"Hush, little man, and I will sing
  Just like a soldier, if I can—
They have a song for everything.
  Listen, my little man!

"This is the soldiers' marching song:
  We'll play this is the village street—"

"Yes, but this road is very long,
    And stones have hurt my feet."

"Nay, little pilgrim, up with you!
    And yonder field shall be the town.
I'll show you how the soldiers do
    Who travel up and down.

"They march and sing and march again,
    Not minding all the stones and dust:
They go, (God grant me rest from men!)
    Forward, because they must."

"Mother, I want to go to sleep."
    "No, darling! Here is bread to eat!
(O God, if thou couldst let me weep,
    Or heal my broken feet!)"

                            GRACE HAZARD CONKLING

VIVE LA FRANCE!

Charlotte Holmes Crawford lives in New York and writes for magazines. Other facts in her life could not be ascertained.

"Vive la France!" like Sara Teasdale's "Sons," records the sacrifices, the heroism, and the patriotic devotion of women during the war.

Franceline rose in the dawning gray,
And her heart would dance though she knelt to pray,
For her man Michel had holiday,
   Fighting for France.

She offered her prayer by the cradle-side,
And with baby palms folded in hers she cried:
"If I have but one prayer, dear, crucified
   Christ—save France!

"But if I have two, then by Mary's grace,
Carry me safe to the meeting-place,
Let me look once again on my dear love's face,
   Save him for France!"

She crooned to her boy: "Oh, how glad he'll be,
Little three-months-old, to set eyes on thee!
For, 'Rather than gold, would I give,' wrote he,
   'A son to France.'

"Come, now, be good, little stray *sauterelle*,
For we're going by-by to thy papa Michel,
But I'll not say where, for fear thou wilt tell,
   Little pigeon of France!

"Six days' leave and a year between!
But what would you have? In six days clean,
Heaven was made," said Franceline,
       "Heaven and France."

She came to the town of the nameless name,
To the marching troops in the streets she came,
And she held high her boy like a taper flame
       Burning for France.

Fresh from the trenches and gray with grime,
Silent they march like a pantomime;
"But what need of music? My heart beats time—
       Vive la France!"

His regiment comes. Oh, then where is ne?
"There is dust in my eyes, for I cannot see,—
Is that my Michel to the right of thee,
       Soldier of France?"

Then out of the ranks a comrade fell,—
"Yesterday—'twas a splinter of shell—
And he whispered thy name, did thy poor Michel,
       Dying for France."

The tread of the troops on the pavement throbbed
Like a woman's heart of its last joy robbed,
As she lifted her boy to the flag, and sobbed:
       "*Vive la France!*"

                           CHARLOTTE HOLMES CRAWFORD

THE PALATINE

In the "Dark Ages"

Willa Sibert Cather was born in Virginia. She was educated at the University of Nebraska. For four years she worked on the Pittsburgh *Daily Leader*, and for six years she was associate editor of *McClure's Magazine*. She has published a number of volumes of poetry. One of her best-known books is "My Antonia." She now lives in New York City.

"The Palatine" is both dramatic and pictorial. "Whole centuries of folly, noise, and sin" sweep by as we read the eager questions of the Saxon boy, safe at home, and the reluctant answers of "big brother," who has travelled widely and seen the desolations of war.

"Have you been with the King to Rome,
    Brother, big brother?"
"I've been there and I've come home.
    Back to your play, little brother."

"Oh, how high is Cæsar's house
    Brother, big brother?"
"Goats about the doorways browse;
Night-hawks nest in the burnt roof-tree.
Home of the wild bird and home of the bee,
A thousand chambers of marble lie
Wide to the sun and the wind and the sky.
Poppies we find amongst our wheat
Grow on Cæsar's banquet-seat.
Cattle crop and neat-herds drowse
On the floors of Cæsar's house."

"But what has become of Cæsar's gold,
    Brother, big brother?"

"The times are bad and the world is old—
Who knows the where of the Cæsar's gold?
Night comes black o'er the Cæsar's hill;
The wells are deep and the tales are ill;
Fireflies gleam in the damp and mould—
All that is left of the Cæsar's gold.
    Back to your play, little brother."

"What has become of the Cæsar's men,
    Brother, big brother?"
"Dogs in the kennel and wolf in the den
Howl for the fate of the Cæsar's men.
Slain in Asia, slain in Gaul,
By Dacian border and Persian wall.
Rhineland orchard and Danube fen
Fatten their roots on Cæsar's men."

"Why is the world so sad and wide,
    Brother, big brother?"
"Saxon boys by their fields that bide
Need not know if the world is wide.
Climb no mountain but Shere-end Hill,
Cross no water but goes to mill.
Ox in the stable and cow in the byre,
Smell of the wood-smoke and sleep by the fire;
Sun-up in seed-time—a likely lad
Hurts not his head that the world is sad.
    Back to your play, little brother."

WILLA SIBERT CATHER

THE OLD HOUSES OF FLANDERS

Ford Madox Ford is the grandson of a celebrated British painter, Ford Madox Brown. He has written fiction and essays and several volumes of poetry. Of late his biography of the novelist Conrad, of whom he was a close friend, has stirred much controversy.

The loss of human life was so appalling during the World War that we gave little thought to other losses. But there were other losses. As W. H. Ogilvie in his poem "Canadians" has sympathetically described the horses on their way to the battle-fields, so Ford Madox Ford has pictured the destruction of the houses of Flanders among the flames of war. The human quality of these houses makes them very appealing as they perish, and in perishing symbolize the ending of an era.

The old houses of Flanders,
They watch by the high cathedrals;
They overtop the high town halls;
They have eyes, mournful, tolerant and sardonic, for
        ways of men
In the high, white-tiled gables.
The rain and the night have settled down on Flanders;
It is all wet darkness; you can see nothing.

Then those old eyes, mournful, tolerant and sardonic,
Look at great, sudden, red lights,
Look upon the shades of the cathedrals;
And the golden rods of the illuminated rain,
For a second . . .

And those old eyes,
Very old eyes that have watched the ways of men for many
        generations,
Close forever.

The high, white shoulders of the gables
Slouch together for a consultation,
Slant drunkenly over in the lea of the flaming cathedrals.
They are no more, the old houses of Flanders.

FORD MADOX FORD

PRINCETON

Alfred Noyes is an English poet born in Staffordshire and educated at Oxford. Poetry has always been his profession. He
was made professor of Modern English Literature at Princeton
University in 1914. He has written many stirring poems having
to do with England's past. During the World War he served in
the British Foreign Office.

"Princeton" begins with a quatrain written for a monument
which marks the grave in which American and British soldiers
were buried after one of the bloody contests of the Revolutionary
War. The ghostly figure of Washington utters the prayer of all
of us for "a world set free from wars."

> Here Freedom stood by slaughtered friend and foe,
> And, ere the wrath paled or that sunset died,
> Looked through the ages; then, with eyes aglow,
> Laid them to wait that future, side by side.

Now lamp-lit gardens in the blue dusk shine
  Through dogwood, red and white;
And round the gray quadrangles, line by line,
  The windows fill with light,
Where Princeton calls to Magdalen, tower to tower,
  Twin lanthorns of the law;
And those cream-white magnolia boughs embower
  The halls of Old Nassau.

The dark bronze tigers crouch on either side
  Where redcoats used to pass;
And round the bird-loved house where Mercer died,
  And violets dusk the grass,
By Stony Brook that ran so red of old,
  But sings of friendship now,
To feed the old enemy's harvest fiftyfold
  The green earth takes the flow.

Through this May night, if one great ghost should stray
    With deep remembering eyes,
Where that old meadow of battle smiles away
    Its blood-stained memories,
If Washington should walk where friend and foe
    Sleep and forget the past,
Be sure his unquenched heart would leap to know
    Their souls are linked at last.

Be sure, he walks, in shadowy buff and blue,
    Where these dim lilacs wave.
He bends his head to bless, as dreams come true,
    The promise of that grave;
Then, with a vaster hope than thought can scan,
    Touching his ancient sword,
Prays for that mightier realm of God in man:
    "Hasten Thy kingdom, Lord.

"Land of our hope, land of the singing stars,
    Type of the world to be,
The vision of a world set free from wars
    Takes life, takes form from thee;
Where all the jarring nations of this earth,
    Beneath the all-blessing sun,
Bring the new music of mankind to birth,
    And make the whole world one."

And those old comrades rise around him there,
    Old foemen, side by side,
With eyes like stars upon the brave night air,
    And young as when they died,
To hear your bells, O beautiful Princeton towers,
    Ring for the world's release.
They see you piercing like gray swords through flowers,
    And smile, from souls at peace.

ALFRED NOYES

THE RED CROSS SPIRIT SPEAKS

John Finley, born at Grand Ridge, Illinois, was educated at
Knox College. He was given the degree of LL.D. by Park College, Knox, the University of Wisconsin, Princeton, Tulane,
Williams, Dartmouth, and Brown. The degree of L.H.D. was
conferred by Colgate and the University of New York. He has
been president of three colleges, Commissioner of Education of
the State of New York, and associate editor of the New York
Times. During the World War he was commander of the American Red Cross for Palestine and the Near East. He has been
given decorations by Japan, France, Italy, and Servia. He has
been crowned by the Acadèmie Française. His books are mainly
sociological and historical.

> Wherever war with its red woes,
> Or flood, or fire, or famine goes,
>   There, too, go I;
> If earth in any quarter quakes
> Or pestilence its ravage makes,
>   Thither I fly.

> I kneel behind the soldier's trench,
> I walk 'mid shambles' smear and stench,
>   The dead I mourn;
> I bear the stretcher and I bend
> O'er Fritz and Pierre and Jack to mend
>   What shells have torn.

> I go wherever men may dare,
> I go wherever woman's care
>   And love can live,
> Wherever strength and skill can bring
> Surcease to human suffering,
>   Or solace give.

I helped upon Haldora's shore;
With Hospitaller Knights I bore
    The first red cross;
I was the Lady of the Lamp;
I saw in Solferino's camp
    The crimson loss.

I am your pennies and your pounds;
I am your bodies on their rounds
    Of pain afar;
I am *you*, doing what you would,
If you were only where you could—
    Your avatar.

The cross which on my arm I wear,
The flag which o'er my breast I bear,
    Is but the sign
Of what you'd sacrifice for him
Who suffers on the hellish rim
    Of war's red line.

JOHN FINLEY

THE BELLS OF PEACE

John Galsworthy is a famous English novelist, dramatist, and essayist. He has published one volume of verse, and is the author of the "Forsyte Saga."

Lilies are here, tall in the garden-bed,
And on the moor are still the buds of May;
Roses are here—and, tolling for our dead,
The bells of Peace make summer holiday.

Listening? They, who in their Springtime went?
The young, the brave dead, leaving all behind,
All of their home, love, laughter, and content,
The village sweetness and the Western wind.

Leaving the quiet trees and the cattle red,
The Southern soft mist over granite tor—
Whispered from life, by secret valor led
To face the horror that their souls abhor.

Here in the starlight to the owl's "'To-whoo!'"
They wandered once—they wander still, maybe,
Dreaming of home, clinging the long night through
To sound and sight fastened in memory.

Here in the sunlight and the bracken green—
Wild happy roses starring every lane—
Eager to reach the good that might have been,
They *were* at peace. Are they at peace again?

Bells of remembrance, on this summer eve
Of our relief, Peace and Good-will ring in!
Ring out the Past, and let not Hate bereave
Our dreaming dead of all they died to win!

JOHN GALSWORTHY

EVERYONE SANG

Siegfried Sassoon was born in England and educated at Cambridge. In the World War he was a captain in the Royal Welsh Fusiliers. He fought in France and Palestine and won the Military Cross for bringing the wounded from the battle-field. His poetry since the war is devoted to attacks on its unnecessary horror and waste. John Masefield, referring to his poetry before the war, has called him "one of England's most brilliant rising stars," and John Gould Fletcher speaks of the "swooning loveliness of Sassoon."

"Everyone Sang" voices lyrically the joy that swept over the world when the Armistice was signed.

Everyone suddenly burst out singing;
And I was filled with such delight
As prisoned birds must find in freedom,
Winging wildly across the white
Orchards and dark-green fields; on—on—and
    out of sight.

Everyone's voice was suddenly lifted;
And beauty came like the setting sun:
My heart was shaken with tears; and horror
Drifted away . . . O, but Everyone
Was a bird; and the song was wordless; the
    singing will never be done.

                                    SIEGFRIED SASSOON

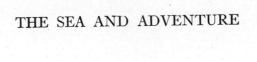

THE SEA AND ADVENTURE

SEA–FEVER

John Masefield was born in England. He was apprenticed as
a cabin-boy at fourteen and spent several years at sea. He
worked in New York as a bartender and a factory hand. He
was working in a restaurant in Yonkers when he stumbled on a
volume of Chaucer and decided to write. He returned to England and devoted himself to poetry. He has published several
novels and many volumes of poetry and plays. During the World
War he served with the Red Cross in France and at Gallipoli,
fitting out a hospital-ship at his own expense.

We have spoken elsewhere of Masefield's love of the sea.
Here again are the rhythms of the sea and the wind and the
songs of sailors.

I must go down to the seas again, to the lonely sea and the
    sky,
And all I ask is a tall ship and a star to steer her by,
And the wheel's kick and the wind's song and the white sail's
    shaking,
And a gray mist on the sea's face, and a gray dawn breaking.

I must go down to the seas again, for the call of the running
    tide
Is a wild call and a clear call that may not be denied;
And all I ask is a windy day with the white clouds flying,
And the flung spray and the blown spume, and the sea-gulls
    crying.

I must go down to the seas again, to the vagrant gypsy life,
To the gull's way and the whale's way where the wind's like
    a whetted knife;
And all I ask is a merry yarn from a laughing fellow-rover,
And quiet sleep and a sweet dream when the long trick's over.

                                        JOHN MASEFIELD

THE SEA GYPSY

Richard Hovey was born at Normal, Illinois. He is a well-known dramatist and poet. He wrote "Songs from Vagabondia" with Bliss Carman. He died in 1900.

I am fevered with the sunset,
  I am fretful with the bay,
For the wander-thirst is on me
  And my soul is in Cathay.

There's a schooner in the offing,
  With her topsails shot with fire,
And my heart has gone aboard her
  For the Islands of Desire.

I must forth again to-morrow!
  With the sunset I must be
Hull down on the trail of rapture
  In the wonder of the sea.

RICHARD HOVEY

HARBURY

Louise Driscoll was born in Poughkeepsie, New York. She began writing at sixteen and has produced much fiction and poetry. In 1914 her poem "Metal Checks" won the hundred-dollar prize offered by *Poetry, A Magazine of Verse*.

"Harbury" dramatically describes the fascination the sea exerts over the people who earn their livelihood by it and suffer by it.

All the men of Harbury go down to the sea in ships,
The wind upon their faces, the salt upon their lips.

The little boys of Harbury, when they are laid to sleep,
Dream of masts and cabins and the wonders of the deep.

The women-folk of Harbury have eyes like the sea,
Wide with watching wonder, deep with mystery.

I met a woman: "Beyond the bar," she said,
"Beyond the shallow water where the green lines spread,

"Out beyond the sand-bar and the white spray,
My three sons wait for the Judgment Day."

I saw an old man who goes to sea no more,
Watch from morn to evening down on the shore.

"The sea's a hard mistress," the old man said;
"The sea is always hungry and never full fed.

"The sea had my father and took my son from me—
Sometimes I think I see them, walking on the sea!

"I'd like to be in Harbury on the Judgment Day,
When the word is spoken and the sea is wiped away,

"And all the drowned fisher-boys with seaweed in their hair,
Rise and walk to Harbury to meet the women there.

"I'd like to be in Harbury to see the souls arise,
Son and mother hand in hand, lovers with glad eyes

"I think there would be many who would turn and look
  with me,
Hoping for another glimpse of the cruel sea!

"They tell me that in Paradise the fields are green and still;
With pleasant flowers everywhere that all may take who will,

"And four great rivers flowing from out the throne of God
That no one ever drowns in and souls may cross dry-shod.

"I think among those wonders there will be men like me
Who miss the old salt danger of the singing sea.

"For in my heart, like some old shell, inland, safe, and dry,
Any one who harks will still hear the sea cry."

LOUISE DRISCOLL

THE GRAVEDIGGER

For the biographical sketch of Bliss Carman, see "Lord of My Heart's Elation."

"The Gravedigger" will not reveal the full value of its "s" and "o" sounds unless it is read aloud. The choice of words is such that we hear the impact of the sea on the shore and the long, rolling cadences of the waves.

Oh, the shambling sea is a sexton old,
And well his work is done.
With an equal grave for lord and knave,
He buries them every one.

Then hoy and rip, with a rolling hip,
He makes for the nearest shore;
And God, who sent him a thousand ship,
Will send him a thousand more;

But some he'll save for a bleaching grave,
And shoulder them in to shore,—
Shoulder them in, shoulder them in,
Shoulder them in to shore.

Oh, the ships of Greece and the ships of Tyre
Went out, and where are they?
In the port they made, they are delayed
With the ships of yesterday.

He followed the ships of England far,
As the ships of long ago;
And the ships of France they led him a dance,
But he laid them all a-row.

Oh, a loafing, idle lubber to him
Is the sexton of the town;
For sure and swift, with a guiding lift,
He shovels the dead men down.

But though he delves so fierce and grim,
His honest graves are wide,
As well they know who sleep below
The dredge of the deepest tide.

Oh, he works with a rollicking stave at lip,
And loud is the chorus skirled;
With the burly rote of his rumbling throat
He batters it down the world.

He learned it once in his father's house,
Where the ballads of eld were sung;
And merry enough is the burden rough,
But no man knows the tongue.

Oh, fair, they say, was his bride to see,
And wilful she must have been,
That she could bide at his gruesome side
When the first red dawn came in.

And sweet, they say, is her kiss to those
She greets to his border home;
And softer than sleep her hand's first sweep
That beckons, and they come.

Oh, crooked is he, but strong enough
To handle the tallest mast;
From the royal bark to the slaver dark,
He buries them all at last.

Then hoy and rip, with a rolling hip,
He makes for the nearest shore;
And God, who sent him a thousand ship,
Will send him a thousand more;

But some he'll save for a bleaching grave,
And shoulder them in to shore—
Shoulder them in, shoulder them in,
Shoulder them in to shore.

BLISS CARMAN

OREAD

For the biographical sketch of H. D., see "Priapus."

"Oread" is an admirable study in imagery. Its cadences suggest wave movements and are five in number: (1) "Whirl up, sea—" (2) "Whirl your pointed pines." (3) "Splash your great pines on our rocks." (4) "Hurl your green over us." (5) "Cover us with your pools of fir."

> Whirl up, sea—
> Whirl your pointed pines.
> Splash your great pines
> On our rocks.
> Hurl your green over us—
> Cover us with your pools of fir.

H. D.

A CARAVAN FROM CHINA COMES
(*After Hafiz*)

For the biographical sketch of Richard Le Gallienne, see "A Ballade-Catalogue of Lovely Things."
This ballad after Hafiz, a Persian poet, is characterized by Oriental imagery and atmosphere.

A caravan from China comes;
　For miles it sweetens all the air
With fragrant silks and dreaming gums,
　Attar and myrrh—
A caravan from China comes.

O merchant, tell me what you bring,
　With music sweet of camel bells;
How long have you been travelling
　With these sweet smells?
O merchant, tell me what you bring.

A lovely lady is my freight,
　A lock escaped of her long hair—
That is this perfume delicate
　That fills the air—
A lovely lady is my freight.

Her face is from another land,
　I think she is no mortal maid,—
Her beauty, like some ghostly hand,
　Makes me afraid;
Her face is from another land.

The little moon my cargo is,
　About her neck the Pleiades
Clasp hands and sing; Hafiz, 'tis this
　Perfumes the breeze—
The little moon my cargo is.

RICHARD LE GALLIENNE

THE GOLDEN JOURNEY TO SAMARKAND

James Elroy Flecker, a young English poet, died in 1915. He was educated at Oxford and by travel on the Continent. He was in the consular service at Beirut, Constantinople, and Smyrna. He published four volumes of poems.

A caravan is always a challenge to our interest, but we generally picture it on its way. Here we see it start from the Gate of the Sun in Bagdad, precious for memories of "The Arabian Nights." At first the poem seems a story of mad adventure for an unknown good; but toward its close we catch a hint of allegory, in which the story of every man's life is written, for each of us feels impelled to make a "golden journey" to some Samarkand of his dreams.

At the Gate of the Sun, Bagdad, in olden time

The Merchants (*together*)

Away, for we are ready to a man!
   Our camels sniff the evening and are glad.
Lead on, O master of the Caravan:
   Lead on the Merchant-Princes of Bagdad.

The Chief Draper

Have we not Indian carpets dark as wine,
   Turbans and sashes, gowns and bows and veils,
And broideries of intricate design,
   And printed hangings in enormous bales?

The Chief Grocer

We have rose-candy, we have spikenard,
   Mastic and terebinth and oil and spice,
And such sweet jams meticulously jarred
   As God's own Prophet eats in Paradise.

THE PRINCIPAL JEWS

And we have manuscripts in peacock styles
  By Ali of Damascus; we have swords
Engraved with storks and apes and crocodiles,
  And heavy beaten necklaces, for Lords.

.   .   .   .

THE MASTER OF THE CARAVAN

But who are ye in rags and rotten shoes,
  You dirty-bearded, blocking up the way?

THE PILGRIMS

We are the Pilgrims, master; we shall go
  Always a little further: it may be
Beyond that last blue mountain barred with snow,
  Across that angry or that glimmering sea.

White on a throne or guarded in a cave
  There lives a prophet who can understand
Why men were born, but surely we are brave,
  Who make the golden journey to Samarkand.

THE CHIEF MERCHANT

We gnaw the nail of hurry. Master, away!

ONE OF THE WOMEN

O turn your eyes to where your children stand.
Is not Bagdad the beautiful? O stay!

THE MERCHANTS (*in chorus*)

We take the Golden Road to Samarkand.

.   .   .   .

A Pilgrim with a Beautiful Voice

Sweet to ride forth at evening from the wells
    When shadows pass gigantic on the sand,
And softly through the silence beat the bells
    Along the golden road to Samarkand.

A Merchant

We travel not for trafficking alone:
    By hotter winds our fiery hearts are fanned:
For lust of knowing what should not be known
    We make the golden journey to Samarkand.

The Master of the Caravan

Open the gate, O watchman of the night!

The Watchman

Ho, travellers, I open. For what land
Leave you the dim-moon city of delight?

The Merchants (*with a shout*)

We make the golden journey to Samarkand.
    (*The Caravan passes through the gate.*)

The Watchman (*consoling the women*)

What would ye, ladies? It was ever thus.
Men are unwise and curiously planned.

A Woman

They have their dreams and do not think of us.

Voices of the Caravan (*in the distance, singing*)

We make the golden journey to Samarkand.

JAMES ELROY FLECKER

THE SANTA FÉ TRAIL—A HUMORESQUE

For the biographical sketch of Vachel Lindsay, see "Pocahontas."

The experiences to which the poet refers in the "Santa Fé Trail" are real. He tramped along the highway, showed to villagers reproductions of his series of drawings, "The Village Improvement Society," recited poems, and was somehow fed. As for the poem itself, perhaps the most remarkable thing about it is this: it consists of three songs extremely different yet perfectly fitted into the rhythmic scheme. The first song is that of noises made by automobiles, through-trains, hand-cars, and names of cities shouted through a megaphone:

> "The United States
> Goes by."

The second song is that of the poet as he philosophizes about possible grasshopper lyrics, talks with the leaves of the mulberry tree, and otherwise communes with the world about him and his own heart. The third song is the bird lyric of the Rachel-Jane in which finally all the other singers of Nature join:

> "Sweet, sweet, sweet, sweet!
> Love and glory, stars and rain,
> Sweet, sweet, sweet, sweet!"

asked the old negro, "What is that bird that sings so well?"
He answered, "That is the Rachel-Jane." "Hasn't it another
name—lark, or thrush, or the like?" "No, jus' Rachel-Jane."

I

In which a Racing Auto comes from the East

This is the order of the music of the morning:—

First, from the far East comes but a crooning;

The crooning turns to a sunrise singing.

Hark to the calm-horn, balm-horn, psalm-horn;

Hark to the faint-horn, quaint-horn, saint-
horn . . .

To be sung delicately to an improvised tune

Hark to the pace-horn, chase-horn, race-horn!
And the holy veil of the dawn has gone,
Swiftly the brazen car comes on.
It burns in the East as the sunrise burns.
I see great flashes where the far trail turns.
Its eyes are lamps like the eyes of dragons.
It drinks gasoline from big red flagons.
Butting through the delicate mists of the morning,
It comes like lightning, goes past roaring.
It will hail all the windmills, taunting, ringing,
Dodge the cyclones,
Count the milestones,
On through the ranges the prairie-dog tills,
Scooting past the cattle on the thousand hills . . .
Ho for the tear-horn, scare-horn, dare-horn,
Ho for the gay-horn, bark-horn, bay-horn.
Ho for Kansas, land that restores us
When houses choke us, and great books bore us!
Sunrise Kansas, harvester's Kansas,
A million men have found you before us.

To be sung or read with great speed

II

In which Many Autos pass Westward

I want live things in their pride to remain.
I will not kill one grasshopper vain
Though he eats a hole in my shirt like a door.
I let him out, give him one chance more.
Perhaps, while he gnaws my hat in his whim,
Grasshopper lyrics occur to him.

In an even, deliberate, narrative manner

I am a tramp by the long trail's border,
Given to squalor, rags and disorder.
I nap and amble and yawn and look,
Write fool-thoughts in my grubby book,

To be read or sung in a rolling bass with some deliberation

Recite to the children, explore at my ease,
Work when I work, beg when I please,
Give crank drawings, that make folks stare,
To the half-grown boys in the sunset-glare;
And get me a place to sleep in the hay
At the end of a live-and-let-live day.

I find in the stubble of the new-cut weeds
A whisper and a feasting, all one needs:
The whisper of the strawberries, white and red,
Here where the new-cut weeds lie dead.
But I would not walk all alone till I die
Without some life-drunk horns going by.
Up round this apple-earth they come,
Blasting the whispers of the morning dumb:—
Cars in a plain realistic row.
And fair dreams fade
When the raw horns blow.

On each snapping pennant
A big black name—
The careering city
Whence each car came.   Like a train-
                                         caller in Union
They tour from Memphis, Atlanta, Savannah,   Depot
Tallahassee and Texarkana.
They tour from St. Louis, Columbus, Manistee,
They tour from Peoria, Davenport, Kankakee.
Cars from Concord, Niagara, Boston,
Cars from Topeka, Emporia and Austin.
Cars from Chicago, Hannibal, Cairo,
Cars from Alton, Oswego, Toledo.
Cars from Buffalo, Kokomo, Delphi,
Cars from Lodi, Carmi, Loami.
Ho for Kansas, land that restores us

When houses choke us, and great books bore us!
While I watch the highroad
And look at the sky,
While I watch the clouds in amazing grandeur
Roll their legions without rain
Over the blistering Kansas plain—
While I sit by the milestone
And watch the sky,
The United States
Goes by!

Listen to the iron horns, ripping, racking.
Listen to the quack horns, slack and clacking!
Way down the road, trilling like a toad,
Here comes the dice-horn, here comes the vice-
    horn,
Here comes the snarl-horn, brawl-horn, lewd-horn,
Followed by the prude-horn, bleak and squeak-
    ing:—
(Some of them from Kansas, some of them from
    Kansas.)
Here comes the hod-horn, plod-horn, sod-horn,
Nevermore-to-roam-horn, loam-horn, home-horn,
(Some of them from Kansas, some of them from
    Kansas.)

*To be given
very harshly
with a snap-
ping explo-
siveness*

> *Far away the Rachel-Jane,*
> *Not defeated by the horns,*
> *Sings amid a hedge of thorns:—*
> *"Love and life,*
> *Eternal youth—*
> *Sweet, sweet, sweet, sweet!*
> *Dew and glory,*

*To be read or
sung well-nigh
in a whisper*

Love and truth,
Sweet, sweet, sweet, sweet!"

While smoke-black freights on the double-tracked
   railroad, *Louder and louder, faster and faster*
Driven as though by the foul-fiend's ox-goad,
Screaming to the west coast, screaming to the east,
Carry off a harvest, bring back a feast,
Harvesting machinery and harness for the beast.
The hand-cars whiz, and rattle on the rails;
The sunlight flashes on the tin dinner-pails.
And then, in an instant, *In a rolling bass with increasing deliberation*
Ye modern men,
Behold the procession once again!
Listen to the iron horns, ripping, racking! *With a snapping explosiveness*
Listen to the wise-horn, desperate-to-advise horn,
Listen to the fast-horn, kill-horn, blast-horn . . .

> *Far away the Rachel-Jane,* *To be sung or read well-nigh in a whisper*
> *Not defeated by the horns,*
> *Sings amid a hedge of thorns:—*
> *"Love and life,*
> *Eternal youth—*
> *Sweet, sweet, sweet, sweet!*
> *Dew and glory,*
> *Love and truth,*
> *Sweet, sweet, sweet, sweet!"*

The mufflers open on a score of cars
With wonderful thunder,
CRACK, CRACK CRACK, *To be brawled in the beginning with a snapping explosiveness ending in languorous chant*
CRACK–CRACK, CRACK–CRACK,
CRACK–CRACK–CRACK, . . .
Listen to the gold-horn . . .

Old-horn . . .
Cold-horn . . .
And all of the tunes, till the night comes down
On hay-stack, and ant-hill, and wind-bitten town.

Then far in the west, as in the beginning,
Dim in the distance, sweet in retreating,
Hark to the faint-horn, quaint-horn, saint-horn,
Hark to the calm-horn, balm-horn, psalm-
    horn . . .

> To be sung to exactly the same whispered tune as the first five lines

They are hunting the goals that they under-
    stand:—
San Francisco and the brown sea-sand.
My goal is the mystery the beggars win.
I am caught in the web the night-winds spin.
The edge of the wheat-ridge speaks to me;
I talk with the leaves of the mulberry tree.
And now I hear, as I sit all alone
In the dusk, by another big Santa-Fé stone,
The souls of the tall corn gathering round,
And the gay little souls of the grass in the ground.
Listen to the tale the cottonwood tells
Listen to the windmills singing o'er the wells.
Listen to the whistling flutes without price
Of myriad prophets out of paradise . . .
Hearken to the wonder that the night-air carries.
Listen . . . to . . . the . . . whisper . . .
Of . . . the . . . prairie . . . fairies
Singing over the fairy plain:
"Sweet, sweet, sweet, sweet!
Love and glory, stars and rain,
Sweet, sweet, sweet, sweet!"

> This section beginning sonorously, ending in a languorous whisper

> To the same whispered tune as the Rachel-Jane song— but very slowly

                              VACHEL LINDSAY

THE AUTOMOBILE

For the biographical sketch of Percy Mackaye, see "Goethals."
In "The Automobile," diction and rhythm combine to hurl
at us the world as seen in panoramic vision from the hurrying
car. Is the hawk's scream one of derision for our senseless hurry?

Fluid the world flowed under us; the hills
    Billow on billow of umbrageous green
    Heaved us, aghast, to fresh horizons, seen
One rapturous instant, blind with flash of rills
And silver-rising storms and dewy stills
    Of dripping boulders, till the dim ravine
    Drowned us again in leafage, whose serene
Coverts grew loud with our tumultuous wills.

Then all of Nature's old amazement seemed
    Sudden to ask us: "Is this also Man?
    This plunging, volant, land-amphibian
What Plato mused and Paracelsus dreamed?
    Reply!" And piercing us with ancient scon
The shrill, primeval hawk gazed down—and screamed.

PERCY MACKAYE

THE HOUSE AND THE ROAD

For the biographical sketch of Josephine Preston Peabody, see
"The Cedars."

The little Road says, Go,
And the little House says, Stay:
And O, it's bonny here at home,
But I must go away.

The little Road, like me,
Would seek and turn and know;
And forth I must, to learn the things
The little Road would show!

And go I must, my dears,
And journey while I may,
Though heart be sore for the little House
That had no word but Stay.

Maybe, no other way
Your child could ever know
Why a little House would have you stay
When a little Road says, Go.

JOSEPHINE PRESTON PEABODY

COMRADES

George Edward Woodberry is the author of much choice poetry. He was long a professor of comparative literature at Columbia. He has had a distinguished career and will always be considered one of the foremost critics of his day. His influence on the younger men of his time has been most marked. He now lives in Beverley, Massachusetts.

Mr. Woodberry's finest work is his sonnets, so critics agree. But no one can fail to enjoy "Comrades," with its fine note of high adventure.

Where are the friends that I knew in my Maying,
    In the days of my youth, in the first of my roaming?
We were dear; we were leal; O, far we went straying;
    Now never a heart to my heart comes homing!—
Where is he now, the dark boy slender
    Who taught me bare-back, stirrup and reins?
I loved him; he loved me; my beautiful, tender
    Tamer of horses on grass-grown plains.

Where is he now whose eyes swam brighter,
    Softer than love, in his turbulent charms;
Who taught me to strike, and to fall, dear fighter,
    And gathered me up in his boyhood arms;
Taught me the rifle, and with me went riding,
    Suppled my limbs to the horseman's war;
Where is he now, for whom my heart's biding,
    Biding, biding—but he rides far!

O love that passes the love of woman!
    Who that hath felt it shall ever forget,
When the breath of life with a throb turns human,
    And a lad's heart is to a lad's heart set?

Ever, forever, lover and rover—
    They shall cling, nor each from other shall part
Till the reign of the stars in the heavens be over,
    And life is dust in each faithful heart.

They are dead, the American grasses under;
    There is no one now who presses my side;
By the African chotts I am riding asunder,
    And with great joy ride I the last great ride.
I am fey; I am fain of sudden dying;
    Thousands of miles there is no one near;
And my heart—all the night it is crying, crying
    In the bosoms of dead lads darling-dear.

Hearts of my music—them dark earth covers;
    Comrades to die, and to die for, were they;
In the width of the world there were no such rovers—
    Back to back, breast to breast, it was ours to stay;
And the highest on earth was the vow that we cherished,
    To spur forth from the crowd and come back never more,
And to ride in the track of great souls perished
    Till the nests of the lark shall roof us o'er.

Yet lingers a horseman on Altai highlands,
    Who hath joy of me, riding the Tartar glissade;
And one, far faring o'er orient islands
    Whose blood yet glints with my blade's accolade;
North, west, east, I fling you my last hallooing,
    Last love to the breasts where my own has bled;
Through the reach of the desert my soul leaps pursuing
    My star where it rises a Star of the Dead.

GEORGE EDWARD WOODBERRY

LEPANTO

For the biographical sketch of Gilbert K. Chesterton, see "The House of Christmas."

"Lepanto" is the story of the conflict between Christians and Turks in 1571. The Turks had taken Cyprus, a victory which so alarmed the Christian world that at the call of Pope Pius V a combined effort was made to check the power of the Sultan and to release the Christian captives who had been enslaved. Don John of Austria, son of Philip II of Spain, was put in command of the fleet of the Holy League, which assembled at Messina. The Turkish and Christian fleets met in battle on the seventh of October. The Turks lost about twenty thousand men, the Christians about eight thousand. This defeat broke forever the naval power of the Turks. A common soldier among the Spanish troops was Cervantes, who was so severely wounded that he lost for life the use of his left hand. This Cervantes was later the creator of Don Quixote, a famous character in literature, intended to make men abhor the "false and absurd stories contained in books of chivalry," and here referred to as "a lean and foolish knight" who "forever rides in vain."

Don John was the last of the Crusaders

"That once went singing southward when all the world was
    young."

"Lepanto" pictures the insolent joy of the Sultan, "the Lord upon the Golden Horn," over his encroachments upon the Christian world; the indifference of England and France to the dangers of Mohammedan conquest, the gallant response of Don John to the call of the Pope; the uneasy stirrings and alarm of Mohammed in Paradise and his call to the Mohammedan angels, Azrael and Ariel, and to all the mysterious hosts of the supernatural world to resist the daring Crusader, Don John. Then Don John looses the cannonade, the Turks are conquered, and the enslaved Christians, chained to the benches of the Turkish galleys, are released and throng up to the decks,

"White for bliss and blind for sun and stunned for liberty."

This splendid ballad stirs reactions of body as well as of mind, when we hear "Dim drums throbbing" and "Strong gongs groaning as the guns boom afar." The refrain is more than a refrain, for it follows the career of Don John from the day he sets forth to the time he "rides homeward with a wreath."

White founts falling in the Courts of the sun,
And the Soldan of Byzantium is smiling as they run;
There is laughter like the fountains in that face of all men feared,
It stirs the forest darkness, the darkness of his beard,
It curls the blood-red crescent, the crescent of his lips,
For the inmost sea of all the earth is shaken with his ships.
They have dared the white republics up the capes of Italy,
They have dashed the Adriatic round the Lion of the Sea,
And the Pope has cast his arms abroad for agony and loss,
And called the kings of Christendom for swords about the Cross.
The cold queen of England is looking in the glass;
The shadow of the Valois is yawning at the Mass;
From evening isles fantastical rings faint the Spanish gun,
And the Lord upon the Golden Horn is laughing in the sun.
Dim drums throbbing, in the hills half heard,
Where only on a nameless throne a crownless prince has stirred,
Where, risen from a doubtful seat and half-attainted stall,
The last knight of Europe takes weapons from the wall,
The last and lingering troubadour to whom the bird has sung,
That once went singing southward when all the world was young.
In that enormous silence, tiny and unafraid,
Comes up along a winding road the noise of the Crusade.
Strong gongs groaning as the guns boom far,
Don John of Austria is going to the war,
Stiff flags straining in the night-blasts cold
In the gloom black-purple, in the glint old-gold,

Torchlight crimson on the copper kettle-drums,
Then the tuckets, then the trumpets, then the cannon, and
    he comes.
Don John laughing in the brave beard curled,
Spurning of his stirrups like the thrones of all the world,
Holding his head up for a flag of all the free.
Love-light of Spain—hurrah!
Death-light of Africa!
Don John of Austria
Is riding to the sea.

Mahound is in his paradise above the evening star,
(*Don John of Austria is going to the war.*)
He moves a mighty turban on the timeless houri's knees,
His turban that is woven of the sunsets and the seas.
He shakes the peacock gardens as he rises from his ease,
And he strides among the tree-tops and is taller than the trees,
And his voice through all the garden is a thunder sent to bring
Black Azrael and Ariel and Ammon on the wing.
Giants and the Genii,
Multiplex of wing and eye,
Whose strong obedience broke the sky
When Solomon was king.

They rush in red and purple from the red clouds of the morn,
From temples where the yellow gods shut up their eyes in
    scorn;
They rise in green robes roaring from the green hells of the
    sea
Where fallen skies and evil hues and eyeless creatures be;
On them the sea-valves cluster and the gray sea-forests curl,
Splashed with a splendid sickness, the sickness of the pearl;

They swell in sapphire smoke out of the blue cracks of the
    ground,—
They gather and they wonder and give worship to Mahound.
And he saith, "Break up the mountains where the hermit-
    folk can hide,
And sift the red and silver sands lest bone of saint abide,
And chase the Giaours flying night and day, not giving rest,
For that which was our trouble comes again out of the west.
We have set the seal of Solomon on all things under sun,
Of knowledge and of sorrow and endurance of things done,
But a noise is in the mountains, in the mountains, and I know
The voice that shook our palaces—four hundred years ago:
It is he that saith not 'Kismet'; it is he that knows not Fate;
It is Richard, it is Raymond, it is Godfrey in the gate!
It is he whose loss is laughter when he counts the wager
    worth,
Put down your feet upon him, that our peace be on the earth."
For he heard drums groaning and he heard guns jar,
(*Don John of Austria is going to the war.*)
Sudden and still—hurrah!
Bolt from Iberia!
Don John of Austria
Is gone by Alcalar.

St. Michael's on his Mountain in the sea-roads of the north
(*Don John of Austria is girt and going forth.*)
Where the gray seas glitter and the sharp tides shift
And the sea-folk labor and the red sails lift.
He shakes his lance of iron and he claps his wings of stone;
The noise is gone through Normandy; the noise is gone alone;
The North is full of tangled things and texts and aching eyes,
And dead is all the innocence of anger and surprise,
And Christian killeth Christian in a narrow dusty room,

And Christian dreadeth Christ that hath a newer face of
    doom,
And Christian hateth Mary that God kissed in Galilee,—
But Don John of Austria is riding to the sea.
Don John calling through the blast and the eclipse
Crying with the trumpet, with the trumpet of his lips.
Trumpet that sayeth *ha!*
      Domino gloria!
Don John of Austria
Is shouting to the ships.

King Philip's in his closet with the Fleece about his neck,
(*Don John of Austria is armed upon the deck.*)
The walls are hung with velvet that is black and soft as sin,
And little dwarfs creep out of it and little dwarfs creep in.
He holds a crystal phial that has colors like the moon,
He touches, and it tingles, and he trembles very soon,
And his face is as a fungus of a leprous white and gray
Like plants in the high houses that are shuttered from the day,
And death is in the phial and the end of noble work,
But Don John of Austria has fired upon the Turk.
Don John's hunting, and his hounds have bayed—
Booms away past Italy the rumor of his raid.
Gun upon gun, ha! ha!
Gun upon gun, hurrah!
Don John of Austria
Has loosed the cannonade.

The Pope was in his chapel before day or battle broke,
(*Don John of Austria is hidden in the smoke.*)
The hidden room in man's house where God sits all the year,
The secret window whence the world looks small and very
    dear.

He sees as in a mirror on the monstrous twilight sea
The crescent of his cruel ships whose name is mystery;
They fling great shadows foe-wards, making Cross and Castle
    dark,
They veil the plumèd lions on the galleys of St. Mark;
And above the ships are palaces of brown, black-bearded
    chiefs,
And below the ships are prisons where with multitudinous
    griefs,
Christian captives sick and sunless, all a laboring race repines
Like a race in sunken cities, like a nation in the mines.
They are lost like slaves that swat, and in the skies of morn-
    ing hung
The stairways of the tallest gods when tyranny was young.
They are countless, voiceless, hopeless as those fallen or flee-
    ing on
Before the high Kings' horses in the granite of Babylon.
And many a one grows witless in his quiet room in hell
Where a yellow face looks inward through the lattice of his
    cell,
And he finds his God forgotten, and he seeks no more a
    sign—
(*But Don John of Austria has burst the battle line!*)
Don John pounding from the slaughter-painted poop,
Purpling all the ocean like a bloody pirate's sloop,
Scarlet running over on the silvers and the golds,
Breaking of the hatches up and bursting of the holds,
Thronging of the thousands up that labor under sea
White for bliss and blind for sun and stunned for liberty.
Vivat Hispania!
Domino Gloria!
Don John of Austria
Has set his people free!

Cervantes on his galley sets the sword back in the sheath
(Don John of Austria rides homeward with a wreath.)
And he sees across a weary land a straggling road in Spain
Up which a lean and foolish knight forever rides in vain
And he smiles, but not as Sultans smile, and settles back the
    blade. . . .
(But Don John of Austria rides home from the Crusade.)

G. K. CHESTERTON

GOD AND MYSTERIES

"GOD, YOU HAVE BEEN TOO GOOD TO ME"

Charles Wharton Stork has been President of the Poetry Society of America and was editor of *Contemporary Verse* for many years. He was born in Philadelphia and educated at Haverford, Harvard, and the University of Pennsylvania. He also studied in the English universities and in the University of Munich. He is an authority on German and Swedish literature.

Poets of to-day often write of God and their spiritual experiences. They speak of joy, mystery, and love, as poets of all times have spoken. But they have something which is distinctly characteristic of our times: a sense of daring intimacy with divine things. In Charles Wharton Stork's poem, "God, You Have Been Too Good to Me," we have the direct approach that a happy child has in addressing his father, whom he loves but does not fear.

> God, You have been too good to me,
> You don't know what You've done.
> A clod's too small to drink in all
> The treasure of the sun.
>
> The pitcher fills the lifted cup
> And still the blessings pour,
> They overbrim the shallow rim
> With cool refreshing store.
>
> You are too prodigal with joy,
> Too careless of its worth,
> To let the stream with crystal gleam
> Fall wasted on the earth.
>
> Let many thirsty lips draw near
> And quaff the greater part!
> There still will be too much for me
> To hold in one glad heart.

CHARLES WHARTON STORK

LORD OF MY HEART'S ELATION

Bliss Carman was born in New Brunswick, Canada, and educated at the University of New Brunswick, the University of
Edinburgh, and Harvard. He was an editor for three years on
the staffs of the New York *Independent* and *The Chap Book*.
Since then he has devoted himself entirely to writing. He lives
in New Canaan, Connecticut.

Near the wild and stormy sea of the North, Bliss Carman
spent his boyhood. To him, as to other poets in their great mo-
ments, the sea became the symbol of the Unknown. So Whittier
sings:

> "I know not where His islands lift
>   Their fronded palms in air;
> I only know I cannot drift
>   Beyond His love and care."

And Tennyson in his last song wrote:

> "Sunset and evening Star,
>   And one clear call for me;
> And may there be no moaning of the bar,
>   When I put out to sea."

> Lord of my heart's elation,
> Spirit of things unseen,
> Be thou my aspiration
> Consuming and serene!

> Bear up, bear out, bear onward,
> This mortal soul alone,
> To selfhood or oblivion,
> Incredibly thine own,—

> As the foamheads are loosened
> And blown along the sea,
> Or sink and merge forever
> In that which bids them be.

I, too, must climb in wonder,
Uplift at thy command,—
Be one with my frail fellows
Beneath the wind's strong hand.

A fleet and shadowy column
Of dust or mountain rain,
To walk the earth a moment
And be dissolved again.

Be thou my exaltation
Or fortitude of mien,
Lord of the world's elation,
Thou breath of things unseen!

                         BLISS CARMAN

LITTLE GRAY SONGS

Number III

Grace Fallow Norton was born in Northfield, Minnesota. She
is a frequent contributor to magazines and the author of several
volumes of poetry. Her home is in Woodstock, New York.

This, the third of a series of poems called "Little Gray Songs
from St. Joseph's," is a beautiful meditation expressing the in-
dividualistic view: it is "God and I."

My little soul I never saw,
Nor can I count its days;
I do not know its wondrous law
And yet I know its ways.

O it is young as morning-hours
And old as is the night;
O it has growth of budding flowers,
Yet tastes my body's blight.

And it is silent and apart,
And far and fair and still,
Yet ever beats within my heart,
And cries within my will.

And it is light and bright and strange,
And sees life far away,
Yet far with near can interchange
And dwell within the day.

My soul has died a thousand deaths,
And yet it does not die;
My soul has broke a thousand faiths,
And yet it cannot lie—

My soul—there's naught can make it less
My soul—there's naught can mar;
Yet here it weeps with loneliness
Within its lonely star.

My soul—not any dark can bind
Nor hinder any hand,
Yet here it weeps—long blind, long blind—
And cannot understand.

GRACE FALLOW NORTON

DEPARTURE

Hermann Hagedorn is an American, a graduate of Harvard
and the author of five volumes of verse.   He is secretary of the
Roosevelt Memorial Association, and has published a book
called "A Boy's Life of Roosevelt."

My true love from her pillow rose
    And wandered down the summer lane.
She left her house to the wind's carouse,
    And her chamber wide to the rain.

She did not stop to don her coat,
    She did not stop to smooth her bed—
But out she went in glad content
    There where the bright path led.

She did not feel the beating storm,
    But fled like a sunbeam, white and frail,
To the sea, to the air, somewhere, somewhere—
    I have not found her trail.

                                HERMANN HAGEDORN

THE BALLAD OF THE CROSS

For the biographical sketch of Theodosia Garrison, see "Shade."

Melchior, Gaspar, Balthazar,
　Great gifts they bore and meet;
White linen for His body fair
　And purple for His feet;
And golden things—the joy of kings—
　And myrrh to breathe Him sweet.

It was the shepherd Terish spake,
　"Oh, poor the gift I bring—
A little cross of broken twigs,
　A hind's gift to a king—
Yet, haply, He may smile to see
　And know my offering."

And it was Mary held her Son
　Full softly to her breast,
"Great gifts and sweet are at Thy feet
　And wonders king-possessed,
O little Son, take Thou the one
　That pleasures Thee the best."

It was the Christ-Child in her arms
　Who turned from gaud and gold,
Who turned from wondrous gifts and great,
　From purple woof and fold,
And to His breast the cross He pressed .
　That scarce his hands could hold.

'Twas king and shepherd went their way—
  Great wonder tore their bliss;
'Twas Mary clasped her little Son
  Close, close to feel her kiss,
And in His hold the cross lay cold
  Between her heart and His!

THEODOSIA GARRISON

A CHRISTMAS FOLK-SONG

Lizette Woodworth Reese was born in Maryland and educated in private schools. Until 1921 she taught in the Western High School of Baltimore. Her books, in order of their publication, are "A Branch of May," "A Handful of Lavender," "A Quiet Road," "A Wayside Lute," and "Spicewood." A fine charm pervades all her work, and she is loved as well as admired.

"A Christmas Folk-Song" has the ballad balance, the "return," and the simplicity of folk-lore.

The little Jesus came to town;
The wind blew up, the wind blew down;
Out in the street the wind was bold;
Now who would house Him from the cold?

Then opened wide a stable door,
Fair were the rushes on the floor;
The Ox put forth a hornèd head;
"Come, little Lord, here make Thy bed."

Uprose the Sheep were folded near;
"Thou Lamb of God, come, enter here."
He entered there to rush and reed,
Who was the Lamb of God indeed.

The little Jesus came to town;
With ox and sheep He laid Him down;
Peace to the byre, peace to the fold,
For that they housed Him from the cold!

LIZETTE WOODWORTH REESE

THE HOUSE OF CHRISTMAS

Gilbert Keith Chesterton was born in London and educated at St. Paul's School and at the Slade School of Art. He is an important figure in the literary life of the twentieth century. He is best known as an epigrammatic essayist. His poems were published in 1915.

There fared a mother driven forth
Out of an inn to roam;
In the place where she was homeless
All men are at home.
The crazy stable close at hand,
With shaking timber and shifting sand,
Grew a stronger thing to abide and stand
Than the square stones of Rome.

For men are homesick in their homes,
And strangers under the sun,
And they lay their heads in a foreign land
Whenever the day is done.
Here we have battle and blazing eyes,
And chance and honor and high surprise,
But our homes are under miraculous skies
Where the Yule tale was begun.

A Child in a foul stable,
Where the beasts feed and foam;
Only where He was homeless
Are you and I at home;
We have hands that fashion and heads that know,
But our hearts we lost—how long ago!
In a place no chart nor ship can show
Under the sky's dome.

This world is wild as an old wives' tale,
And strange the plain things are;
The earth is enough and the air is enough
For our wonder and our war;
But our rest is as far as the fire-drake swings,
And our peace is put in impossible things
Where clashed and thundered unthinkable wings
Round an incredible star.

To an open house in the evening
Home shall men come.
To an older place than Eden
And a taller town than Rome.
To the end of the way of the wandering star,
To the things that cannot be and that are,
To the place where God was homeless
And all men are at home.

GILBERT K. CHESTERTON

A BALLAD OF TREES AND THE MASTER

Sidney Lanier was born at Macon, Georgia. He was a graduate of Oglethorpe College. He was successively a private in the Confederate army, a flute-player in the Peabody Symphony Orchestra, and a lecturer on English at Johns Hopkins University. He died in 1881.

In "A Ballad of Trees and the Master" again the notes of simplicity and intimacy are heard. The repetitions are especially effective, in the first stanza showing exhaustion, in the second renewal of strength.

> Into the woods my Master went,
> Clean forspent, forspent.
> Into the woods my Master came,
> Forspent with love and shame.
> But the olives they were not blind to Him,
> The little gray leaves were kind to Him:
> The thorn-tree had a mind to Him
> When into the woods He came.
>
> Out of the woods my Master went,
> And He was well content.
> Out of the woods my Master came,
> Content with death and shame.
> When Death and Shame would woo Him last,
> From under the trees they drew Him last:
> 'Twas on a tree they slew Him—last
> When out of the woods he came.

SIDNEY LANIER

CHILD

For the biographical sketch of Carl Sandburg, see "Fog."
"Child" is Christ in the temple, talking with the elders.
"Straight and wise" suggests the young sapling; the "tall trees
looking downward, old and gnarled," the learned elders.

The young child, Christ, is straight and wise
And asks questions of the old men, questions
Found under running water for all children,
And found under shadows thrown on still waters
By tall trees looking downward, old and gnarled,
Found to the eyes of children alone, untold,
Singing a low song in the loneliness.
And the young child, Christ, goes on asking
And the old men answer nothing and only know love
For the young child, Christ, straight and wise.

CARL SANDBURG

RETURN

Willard Wattles was born in Kansas and educated in the University of Kansas. He is a teacher of English in the Oregon Agricultural College and lives in Corvallis, Oregon. He has written several volumes of poetry.

The lovely little song "Return" describes the healing of a lame child, and gives his challenging questions and their satisfying answers. The little fellow's confident statement that Jesus will be glad

> "That I've moved into
> His neighborhood"

recalls to us Christ's strongly expressed attitude toward childhood.

Wise man, wise man,
Fingers and thumbs,
Which is the way
That Jesus comes?

Wise man, wise man,
Rabbi, priest,
Did you ever see a man
On such a poor beast?

Wise man, wise man,
I saw a lame child;
And when he came by
Jesus smiled.

Jesus, Jesus,
How do you come?
"To those who are halt
And blind and dumb."

My knee was sprung
And I couldn't see,
So I climbed up high
In a jujube tree.

Jesus, Jesus,
What are you worth?
"The sun and the moon
And the little round earth."

Jesus, Jesus,
Sing me a song.
"I can't stop now,
For the road's too long."

Jesus, Jesus,
Go along, Lord;
My knee is as straight
As the governor's sword.

Jesus, Jesus,
Go along before
To a high house
With a silver door.

But I'll stop first
To clean my feet,
And then sit down
By the chimney-seat.

And Jesus will laugh
And say it's good
That I've moved into
His neighborhood.

                              WILLARD WATTLES

THE DONKEY

For the biographical sketch of Gilbert K. Chesterton, see "The House of Christmas."

In "The Donkey" the grotesque and the holy are contrasted with startling effect. The reference in the last stanza is, of course, to the triumphal entry of Christ into Jerusalem, when palms were strewn before Him.

When fishes flew and forests walked
    And figs grew upon thorn,
Some moment when the morn was blood
    Then surely I was born;

With monstrous head and sickening cry
    And ears like errant wings,
The devil's walking parody
    On all four-footed things.

The tattered outlaw of the earth,
    Of ancient crooked will;
Starve, scourge, deride me: I am dumb,
    I keep my secret still.

Fools! For I also had my hour;
    One far fierce hour and sweet:
There was a shout about my ears,
    And palms before my feet.

                GILBERT KEITH CHESTERTON

I AM THE WIND

Zoë Akins was born in Humansville, Missouri. She was educated at Monticello Seminary, Godfrey, Illinois, and at Hosmer Hall, St. Louis. She is one of the most successful writers of plays in America. Her volume of poems is called "Interpretations'

I am the wind that wavers,
  You are the certain land;
I am the shadow that passes
  Over the sand.

I am the leaf that quivers,
  You the unshaken tree;
You are the stars that are steadfast,
  I am the sea.

You are the light eternal—
  Like a torch I shall die;
You are the surge of deep music,
  I but a cry!

ZOË AKINS

THE MAKING OF BIRDS

Katharine Tynan (Mrs. Hinkson) was born in Dublin and educated in a convent at Drogheda. She is one of the leaders in the Irish literary Renaissance. She is the reviewer of Irish literature for the London *Bookman*. She has published four volumes of poetry and several volumes of fiction. Her two sons served in the British army during the World War, and she did much relief work.

God made Him birds in a pleasant humor;
　　Tired of planets and suns was He.
He said, "I will add a glory to summer,
　　Gifts for my creatures banished from Me!"

He had a thought and it set Him smiling,
　　Of the shape of a bird and its glancing head,
Its dainty air and its grace beguiling:
　　"I will make feathers," the Lord God said.

He made the robin: He made the swallow;
　　His deft hands moulding the shape to His mood,
The thrush and lark and the finch to follow,
　　And laughed to see that His work was good.

He who has given men gift of laughter,
　　Made in his image; He fashioned fit
The blink of the owl and the stork thereafter,
　　The little wren and the long-tailed tit.

He spent in the making His wit and fancies;
　　The wing-feathers He fashioned them strong;
Deft and dear as daisies and pansies,
　　He crowned His work with the gift of song.

"Dearlings," He said, "make songs for my praises!"
  He tossed them loose to the sun and wind,
Airily sweet as pansies and daisies;
  He taught them to build a nest to their mind.

The dear Lord God of His glories weary—
  Christ our Lord had the heart of a boy—
Made Him birds in a moment merry,
  Bade them soar and sing for His joy.

KATHARINE TYNAN

THE MYSTIC

Cale Young Rice was born in Kentucky. He was educated at Cumberland University and at Harvard. He often writes for periodicals and is the author of many volumes of poetry.

There is a quest that calls me,
In nights when I am lone,
The need to ride where the ways divide
The Known from the Unknown.
I mount what thought is near me
And soon I reach the place,
The tenuous rim where the Seen grows dim
And the Sightless hides its face.

I have ridden the wind,
I have ridden the sea,
I have ridden the moon and stars,
I have set my feet on the stirrup-seat
Of a comet coursing Mars.
And everywhere
Thro' the earth and air
My thought speeds, lightning-shod,
It comes to a place where checking pace
It cries, "Beyond lies God!"

It calls me out of the darkness,
It calls me out of sleep,
"Ride! ride! for you must, to the end of Dust!"
It bids and on I sweep
To the wide outposts of Being,
Where there is Gulf alone—
And thro' a Vast that was never passed
I listen for Life's tone.

I have ridden the wind,
I have ridden the night,
I have ridden the ghosts that flee
From the vaults of death like a chilling breath
Over eternity.
And everywhere
Is the earth laid bare—
Ether and star and clod—
Until I wind to its brink and find
But the cry, "Beyond lies God!"

It calls me and ever calls me!
And vainly I reply,
"Fools only ride where the ways divide
What Is from the Whence and Why!"
I'm lifted into the saddle
Of thoughts too strong to tame
And down the deeps and over the steeps
I find—ever the same.

I have ridden the wind,
I have ridden the stars,
I have ridden the force that flies
With far intent thro' the firmament
And each to each allies.
And everywhere
That a thought may dare
To gallop, mine has trod—
Only to stand at last on the strand
Where just beyond lies God.

CALE YOUNG RICE

EACH IN HIS OWN TONGUE

William Herbert Carruth was born in Kansas and educated at the University of Kansas and at Harvard. For some years he was Professor of Comparative Literature and Head of the English Department of Leland Stanford University. He was an authority on the German language, and many of his earlier texts are editions, with notes, of German classics. He published one volume of poetry. He died in 1924.

A fire-mist and a planet,—
  A crystal and a cell,—
A jellyfish and a saurian,
  And caves where cave-men dwell;
Then a sense of law and beauty,
  And a face turned from the clod,—
Some call it Evolution,
  And others call it God.

A haze on the far horizon,
  The infinite, tender sky,
The ripe, rich tints of the cornfields,
  And the wild geese sailing high,—
And all over upland and lowland
  The charm of the goldenrod,—
Some of us call it Autumn,
  And others call it God.

Like tides on a crescent sea-beach,
  When the moon is new and thin,
Into our hearts high yearnings
  Come welling and surging in,—
Come from the mystic ocean,
  Whose rim no foot has trod,—

Some of us call it Longing,
  And others call it God.

A picket frozen on duty,—
  A mother starved for her brood,—
Socrates drinking the hemlock
  And Jesus on the rood;
And millions who, humble and nameless,
  The straight, hard pathway plod,—
Some call it Consecration,
  And others call it God.

                    WILLIAM HERBERT CARRUTH

SWEETWATER RANGE

Lew Sarett, recently professor of English in Northwestern University, has been a woodsman and guide in the Northwest, and has an intimate knowledge of the Chippewa Indians and of the country of which he writes. His books, "Many, Many Moons" and "The Box of God," are among the most important of those that acquaint us with the literature of the American Indian.

I was loping along in the Sweetwater Range,
    When the shadowy clouds of sleep,
On the blue earth had settled like ravens' wings
    With a swift, mysterious sweep.

The Valley lay calm as a beaver-pond
    When the hunter's moon hangs low,
And the hills were soft as the velvet sod
    Under an antelope doe.

Serene overhead in the dusky blue,
    A single star through the night
Glowed like a candle held by God
    As a friendly beacon light.

A flame in the window of His vast house,
    Beckoning out to me—
I could almost see Him peering down,
    As He waited expectantly.

So I flung Him a couple of friendly songs,
    As I cantered a lonely mile;
Swing Low Sweet Chariot, Old Black Joe,
    Jordan, and Beautiful Isle.

For the singing of songs my voice was raw—
   I was never a parson's pet;
And the tremolo wail of a shivering wolf
   Made it a strange duet.

But hard on the echoes—from Avalanche Peak,
   Where the Yellowrock Cataract spills—
I heard Him sing back to me clear as a bell
   In the frosty dawn of the hills.

LEW SARETT

WHAT DIM ARCADIAN PASTURES

Alice Corbin was born in St. Louis. She has been associat
editor of *Poetry, a Magazine of Verse*, since 1912. In 1915 sh
was married to William Penhallow Henderson, the artist. Sh
is the author of a book of dramas for children and of several vo
umes of poetry. She is also the compiler with Harriet Monro
of an anthology called "The New Poetry."

Arcadia in literature is an ideal country where shepherds ar
shepherdesses live simply and happily, in sympathy with th
fauns and dryads.

What dim Arcadian pastures
  Have I known
That suddenly, out of nothing,
  A wind is blown,
Lifting a veil and a darkness,
  Showing a purple sea—
And under your hair the faun's eyes
  Look out on me?

                        ALICE CORBIN

SHEEP AND LAMBS

For the biographical sketch of Katharine Tynan, see "The
Making of Birds."

All in the April morning,
  April airs were abroad;
Sheep with their little lambs
  Passed me by on the road.

The sheep with their little lambs
  Passed me by on the road;
All in the April morning,
  I thought on the Lamb of God.

The lambs were weary, and crying
  With a weak human cry,
I thought on the Lamb of God,
  Going meekly to die.

Up in the blue, blue mountains
  Dewy pastures are sweet;
Rest for the little bodies,
  Rest for the little feet.

Rest for the Lamb of God
  Upon the hill-top green,
Only a cross of shame
  Two stark crosses between.

All in the April evening,
  April airs were abroad,
I saw the sheep with their lambs,
  And thought on the Lamb of God.

KATHARINE TYNAN

TO A TREE IN BLOOM

For the biographical sketch of Hildegarde Flanner, see "Daphne."

There is no silence lovelier than the one
That flowers upon a flowering tree at night.
There is no stillness known beneath the sun
That is so strange to bear, nor half so white.
If I had all that silence in my heart,
What yet unfinished heavens I could sing!
My words lift up and tremble to depart,
Then die in air, from too much uttering.
It must have been beneath a tree like this
An angel sought a girl in Gaiilee,
While she looked up and pondered how the kiss
Of God had come with wings and mystery.
It may be that a single petal fell,
Heavy with sorrow that it could not tell.

                         HILDEGARDE FLANNER

LIFE AND LOVE

A PARTING GUEST

For the biographical sketch of James Whitcomb Riley, see
"When the Frost Is on the Punkin."

What delightful hosts are they—
  Life and Love!
Lingeringly I turn away,
  This late hour, yet glad enough
They have not withheld from me
  Their high hospitality.
So, with face lit with delight
  And all gratitude, I stay
  Yet to press their hands and say,
"Thanks.—So fine a time! Good night."

JAMES WHITCOMB RILEY

LOVE AND LIBERATION

For the biographical sketch of John Hall Wheelock, see
"The Lion House."

Lift your arms to the stars
　　And give an immortal shout;
Not all the veils of darkness
　　Can put your beauty out!

You are armed with love, with love,
　　Nor all the powers of Fate
Can touch you with a spear—
　　Nor all the hands of hate.

What of Good and Evil—
　　Hell and Heaven above?
Trample them with love!
　　Ride over them with love!

JOHN HALL WHEELOCK

DANCE FIGURE

For the Marriage in Cana of Galilee

Ezra Pound was born at Haily, Idaho. He attended Hamilton College and the University of Pennsylvania. He has dwelt much abroad and now lives in London. He is the author of many poems and is a student of French, Chinese, and Hebraic poetry. "Dance Figure" is beautiful in its pattern, which is as varied as the dance, and Oriental in its descriptions and imagery.

Dark-eyed,
O woman of my dreams,
Ivory sandalled,
There is none like thee among the dancers,
None with swift feet.

I have not found thee in the tents,
In the broken darkness.
I have not found thee at the well-head
Among the women with pitchers.

Thine arms are as a young sapling under the bark;
Thy face as a river with lights.

White as an almond are thy shoulders;
As new almonds stripped from the husk.

They guard thee not with eunuchs;
Not with bars of copper.
Gilt turquoise and silver are in the place of thy rest.
A brown robe, with threads of gold woven in patterns,
        hast thou gathered about thee,
O Nathat-Ikanaie, "Tree-at-the-river."

As a rillet among the sedge are thy hands upon me;
Thy fingers a frosted stream.

Thy maidens are white like pebbles:
Their music about thee!

There is none like thee among the dancers;
None with swift feet.

EZRA POUND

THE VASE

Grace Shoup was born in Cambridge, Illinois. She is a graduate of Indiana University and has studied in Eastern universities and in art schools. She has been connected with several newspapers and publishing houses and has written short stories and verse for magazines. She is now teaching in Shortridge High School, Indianapolis.

"The Vase" is a decorative study which reflects Oriental influence. The second stanza records the effect of the vase on the desert horsemen and the jackals. The fourth stanza by three comparisons marks the appearance of the vase in its desert setting.

A great stone vase
Stands in the desert
    Outside the city of Ming,
      A-li-eh-ta,
        Beloved One!

The wild desert horsemen
Trail their spears
    When they pass it;
    The jackals of night
      Sing to it
Their harsh, unmelodious music,
      A-li-eh-ta,
        Beloved One!

A king, long dead,
Once built it,
      To a queen,
    Long faded and gone,
      A-li-eh-ta,
        Beloved One!

It is higher
Than our city gates;
It is gray-green,
Duller than jade;
The winds of the desert
Have worn it
Smoother than ivory,
A-li-eh-ta,
Beloved One!

The stars burn,
Heaven's joss-sticks,
Above it at night;—
And at dawn
I myself have seen
The king's love,
Like a tall spray of
Delicate blossoms,
In that vase in the desert,
Outside the city of Ming,
A-li-eh-ta
Beloved One!

GRACE SHOUP

WHO LOVES THE RAIN

Mrs. Shaw's biography has been given in connection with
"The Harp of the Wind."

The repeated cadences of "Who Loves the Rain" are as sooth-
ing as a gentle rain, a sheltered fireside, the companionship of a
strong soul. To get their effects one should read the poem aloud.

Who loves the rain
And loves his home,
And looks on life with quiet eyes,
Him will I follow through the storm;
And at his hearth-fire keep me warm;
Nor hell nor heaven shall that soul surprise,
Who loves the rain,
And loves his home,
And looks on life with quiet eyes.

FRANCES SHAW

SOMETIMES

Thomas S. Jones, Jr., was born in Boonville, New York. He is now associate editor of *The Pathfinder*. He is the author of "The Rose-Jar" and "The Voice in the Silence." He also contributes to leading magazines.

Across the fields of yesterday
He sometimes comes to me,
A little lad just back from play—
The lad I used to be.

And yet he smiles so wistfully
Once he has crept within,
I wonder if he hopes to see
The man I might have been.

THOMAS S. JONES, JR.

AN OLD WOMAN OF THE ROADS

Padraic Colum was born in Longford, Ireland. He was editor of *The Irish Review* and one of the founders of the Abbey Theatre. He came to America in 1914. He is a lecturer, a playwright, and an author of fairy-tales.

The old woman of the roads is a pathetic figure unfamiliar to Americans. In Ireland such wanderers are now less frequently seen, although formerly only too numerous because of the scarcity of houses and the eviction laws which sent a peasant adrift if failing crops made it impossible to pay his rent. The poem is a true interpretation of a woman's heart. She likes to have "her own things" about her, to give her a sense of permanence in a world where impermanence is often her tragedy. With characteristic Irish tenderness, the writer symbolizes home by what is dear to the woman, "hearth" and "turf" and "clock" and "delph."

O, to have a little house!
To own the hearth and stool and all!
The heaped-up sods upon the fire,
The pile of turf against the wall!

To have a clock with weights and chains
And pendulum swinging up and down!
A dresser filled with shining delph,
Speckled and white and blue and brown!

I could be busy all the day
Clearing and sweeping hearth and floor,
And fixing on their shelf again
My white and blue and speckled store!

I could be quiet there at night
Beside the fire and by myself,
Sure of a bed and loath to leave
The ticking clock and the shining delph!

Och! but I'm weary of mist and dark,
And roads where there's never a house nor bush,
And tired I am of bog and road,
And the crying wind and the lonesome hush!

And I am praying to God on high,
And I am praying Him night and day,
For a little house—a house of my own—
Out of the wind's and the rain's way.

PADRAIC COLUM

AFTER SUNSET

Grace Hazard Conkling (née Hazard) was born in New York City. She was educated at Smith College and at Harvard Summer School, and studied language and music at the University of Heidelberg and in Paris. She is now a professor of English at Smith.

The quiet, restful assurance of the hills reminds us of the promise, "Underneath are the Everlasting Arms." It is worth while to prove by the poem that the author has indeed "an understanding with the hills."

I have an understanding with the hills
At evening, when the slanted radiance fills
Their hollows, and the great winds let them be,
And they are quiet and look down at me.
Oh, then I see the patience in their eyes
Out of the centuries that made them wise.
They lend me hoarded memory, and I learn
Their thoughts of granite and their whims of fern,
And why a dream of forests must endure
Though every tree be slain; and how the pure,
Invisible beauty has a word so brief,
A flower can say it, or a shaken leaf,
But few may ever snare it in a song,
Though for the quest a life is not too long.
When the blue hills grow tender, when they pull
The twilight close with gesture beautiful,
And shadows are their garments, and the air
Deepens, and the wild veery is at prayer,
Their arms are strong around me; and I know
That somehow I shall follow when they go
To the still land beyond the evening star,
Where everlasting hills and valleys are,
And silence may not hurt us any more,
And terror shall be past, and grief and war.

GRACE HAZARD CONKLING

COMING TO PORT

Max Eastman was born at Canandaigua, New York. He was graduated from Williams College and for a time taught at Columbia University. He has written several volumes of poetry and a valuable criticism called "Enjoyment of Poetry."

In "Coming to Port"—which should, by all means, be read aloud—the gentle, slow pulsations of the ship as it prepares to enter port are perceptible both in the diction and the rhythm.

Our motion on the soft still misty river
Is like rest; and like the hours of doom
That rise and follow one another ever,
Ghosts of sleeping battle-cruisers loom
And languish quickly in the liquid gloom.

From watching them your eyes in tears are gleaming,
And your heart is still; and like a sound
In silence is your stillness in the streaming
Of light-whispered laughter all around,
Where happy passengers are homeward bound.

Their sunny journey is in safety ending,
But for you no journey has an end;
The tears that to your eyes their light are lending
Shine in softness to no waiting friend;
Beyond the search of any eye they tend.

There is no nest for the unresting fever
Of your passion, yearning, hungry-veined;
There is no rest nor blessedness forever
That can clasp you, quivering and pained,
Whose eyes burn forward to the unattained.

Like time, and like the river's fateful flowing,
Flowing though the ship has come to rest,
Your love is passing through the mist and going,
Going infinitely from your breast,
Surpassing time on its immortal quest.

The ship draws softly to the place of waiting,
All flush forward with a joyful aim,
And while their hands with happy hands are mating,
Lips are laughing out a happy name—
You pause, and pass among them like a flame.

MAX EASTMAN

FROST TO–NIGHT

Edith M. Thomas was born at Chatham, Ohio, but spent most of her life in New York. She devoted her life to literature as editor and poet and was the author of ten volumes of lyrics.

"Frost To-night" is a parable of conservative form and great beauty of expression. The world dearly loves a parable, for it teaches truth in terms of the imagination. We recall that Christ used it constantly to convey His divine messages. "And in . . . parables spake he unto them . . . and without a parable spake he not unto them."

Apple-green west and an orange bar,
And the crystal eye of a lone, one star . . .
And "Child, take the shears and cut what you will,
Frost to-night—so clear and dead-still."

Then I sally forth, half sad, half proud,
And I come to the velvet, imperial crowd,
The wine-red, the gold, the crimson, the pied —
The dahlias that reign by the garden-side.

The dahlias I might not touch till to-night!
A gleam of the shears in the fading light,
And I gathered them all,—the splendid throng,
And in one great sheaf I bore them along.

In my garden of Life with its all-late flowers
I heed a Voice in the shrinking hours:
"Frost to-night—so clear and dead-still" . . .
Half sad, half proud, my arms I fill.

EDITH M. THOMAS

STANDARDS

The biography of Mr. Stork will be found in connection with
God, You Have Been Too Good to Me."
"Standards," as short as it is, is a study in psychology and art.

White is the skimming gull on the sombre green of the fir-
trees,
Black is the soaring gull on a snowy glimmer of cloud.

CHARLES WHARTON STORK

I AM WEARY OF BEING BITTER

Arthur Davison Ficke was born in Davenport, Iowa, where
he still lives. He graduated from Harvard and later studied law
in the University of Iowa. He served in France in the Ordnance
Department until 1919, with the rank of lieutenant-colonel. He
is the author of several volumes of poetry.

In "I Am Weary of Being Bitter" the power of song is seri
ously and beautifully expressed. The theme reminds us of "A
Song for St. Cecilia's Day," in which Dryden says,

> "From harmony, from heavenly harmony,
> This universal frame began."

But Mr. Ficke has affirmed his belief in the magic and wisdom
of song, in the simpler, less affected diction of to-day.

I am weary of being bitter and weary of being wise,
    And the armor and the mask of these fall from me, after
      long.
I would go where the islands sleep, or where the sea-dawns
    rise,
    And lose my bitter wisdom in the wisdom of a song.

There are magics in melodies, unknown of the sages;
    The powers of purest wonder on secret wings go by.
Doubtless out of the silence of dumb preceding ages
    Song woke the chaos-world—and light swept the sky.

All that we know is idle; idle is all we cherish;
    Idle the will that takes loads that proclaim it strong.
For the knowledge, the strength, the burden—all shall perish
    One thing only endures, one thing only—song.

ARTHUR DAVISON FICKE

CINQUAINS

Adelaide Crapsey was born in Rochester, New York. After being graduated from Vassar College, she taught for a time in Smith College and later studied archæology abroad. She published two volumes of poetry and "A Study in English Metrics." She died in 1914.

The cinquain—a poem of five lines—is a pattern devised by Miss Crapsey. No doubt her study of the Japanese "hakku," a poem of seventeen syllables, somewhat influenced her choice of a pattern. But in essentials it is her own. The usual plan is this: the first line has two syllables; the second, four; the third, six; the fourth, eight; and the fifth line by using only two syllables makes a sharp "return." The symbols and the emotion in these poems are both lovely and satisfying.

FATE DEFIED
As it
Were tissue of silver
I'll wear, O fate, thy gray,
And go, mistily radiant, clad
Like the moon.

NOVEMBER NIGHT
Listen . . .
With faint dry sound,
Like steps of passing ghosts,
The leaves, frost-crisp'd, break from the trees
And fall.

ADELAIDE CRAPSEY

MY WAGE

Jessie B. Rittenhouse was born in Mt. Morris, New York. She is a graduate of Genesee Wesleyan Seminary. In 1924 she was married to Clinton Scollard, the poet. She is the author of "The Door of Dreams" and "The Lifted Cup," besides several distinguished anthologies.

I bargained with Life for a penny,
    And Life would pay no more,
However I begged at evening
    When I counted my scanty store;

For Life is a just employer,
    He gives you what you ask,
But once you have set the wages,
    Why, you must bear the task.

I worked for a menial's hire,
    Only to learn, dismayed,
That any wage I had asked of Life,
    Life would have paid.

JESSIE B. RITTENHOUSE

BARTER

Sara Teasdale (Mrs. Filsinger) was born in St. Louis. She was educated in private schools and by travel abroad. She is the author of a number of volumes of poetry and has published two anthologies. She now lives in New York City. She is considered our foremost writer of lyrics. John Gould Fletcher speaks of "the frail, delicate intensity" of her songs.

To choose among Sara Teasdale's poems is difficult; one wants to gather them by handfuls, as Aladdin gathered jewels in the mysterious cave. Her poems all report truly and sincerely her thoughts and her reactions to "stars above and earth below." They are also marvels of craftsmanship.

Life has loveliness to sell,
    All beautiful and splendid things,
Blue waves whitened on a cliff,
    Soaring fire that sways and sings,
And children's faces looking up
Holding wonder like a cup.

Life has loveliness to sell,
    Music like a curve of gold,
Scent of pine trees in the rain,
    Eyes that love you, arms that hold,
And for your spirit's still delight,
Holy thoughts that star the night.

                                SARA TEASDALE

SOULS

Fannie Stearns Davis (Mrs. Gifford) was born in Cleveland, Ohio. She is a graduate of Smith College. Her home is in Pittsfield, Massachusetts.

My soul goes clad in gorgeous things,
    Scarlet and gold and blue.
And at her shoulder sudden wings
    Like long flames flicker through.

And she is swallow-fleet, and free
    From mortal bonds and bars.
She laughs, because eternity
    Blossoms for her with stars!

O folk who scorn my stiff grav gown,
    My dull and foolish face,
Can ye not see my soul flash down,
    A singing flame through space?

And folk, whose earth-stained looks I hate,
    Why may I not divine
Your souls, that must be passionate,
    Shining and swift, as mine?

FANNIE STEARNS DAVIS

STAINS

Theodosia Garrison's biography is given in connection with
he poem "Shade."
"Stains" has a dramatic quality which gives beauty and em-
phasis to the theme, the ravages of sin cannot be concealed.
"Naked the soul goes up to God."

> The three ghosts on the lonesome road
>   Spake each to one another,
> "Whence came that stain about your mouth
>   No lifted hand may cover?"
> "From eating of forbidden fruit,
>   Brother, my brother."
>
> The three ghosts on the sunless road
>   Spake each to one another,
> "Whence came that red burn on your foot
>   No dust or ash may cover?"
> "I stamped a neighbor's hearth flame out,
>   Brother, my brother."
>
> The three ghosts on the windless road
>   Spake each to one another,
> "Whence came that blood upon your hand
>   No other hand may cover?"
> "From breaking of a woman's heart,
>   Brother, my brother."
>
> "Yet on the earth clean men we walked,
>   Glutton and Thief and Lover;
> White flesh and fair it hid our stains
>   That no man might discover."
> "Naked the soul goes up to God,
>   Brother, my brother."
>   THEODOSIA GARRISON

A LIFE LESSON

For the biographical sketch of James Whitcomb Riley, see "When the Frost Is on the Punkin."

Masefield in "Cargoes" tells the story of commerce and democracy in three stanzas; so Riley tells in equally small space the story of a woman's life tragedies. This poem is marked by fine artistry and true feeling.

> There! little girl; don't cry!
>   They have broken your doll, I know;
>   And your tea-set blue,
>   And your playhouse, too,
>   Are things of the long ago;
>   But childish troubles will soon pass by.—
>   There! little girl; don't cry!
>
> There! little girl; don't cry!
>   They have broken your slate, I know;
>   And the glad, wild ways
>   Of your schoolgirl days
>   Are things of the long ago;
>   But life and love will soon come by.—
>   There! little girl; don't cry!
>
> There! little girl; don't cry!
>   They have broken your heart, I know;
>   And the rainbow gleams
>   Of your youthful dreams
>   Are things of the long ago;
>   But heaven holds all for which you sigh.—
>   There! little girl; don't cry!

JAMES WHITCOMB RILEY

THE FALCONER OF GOD

William Rose Benét was born at Fort Hamilton, New York Harbor. He was educated at Albany Academy, at Sheffield Scientific School, and at Yale. He has been assistant editor of *The Century* and of *The Literary Review* of the New York *Evening Post.* He was commissioned second lieutenant in the United States Air Service (non-flying) in the World War. He is the author of a number of volumes of poetry and a contributor to many magazines.

In "The Falconer of God" the writer describes the quest of the soul for ideal beauty under the symbolism of the solitary hunter who rides beneath the moon, his falcon soaring overhead. The diction of the poem is delicate, sure, compelling. The refrain adds much to the charm.

I flung my soul to the air like a falcon flying.
I said, "Wait on, wait on, while I ride below!
    I shall start a heron soon
    In the marsh beneath the moon—
A strange white heron rising with silver on its wings,
        Rising and crying
    Wordless, wondrous things;
    The secret of the stars, of the world's heart-strings
        The answer to their woe.
Then stoop thou upon him, and grip and hold him so!"

    My wild soul waited on as falcons hover.
    I beat the reedy fens as I trampled past.
    I heard the mournful loon
    In the marsh beneath the moon.
And then with feathery thunder—the bird of my desire
        Broke from the cover
    Flashing silver fire.
High up among the stars I saw his pinions spire.

The pale clouds gazed aghast
As my falcon stooped upon him, and gripped and held him
   fast.

My soul dropped through the air—with heavenly plunder?—
Gripping the dazzling bird my dreaming knew?
   Nay! but a piteous freight,
   A dark and heavy weight
Despoiled of silver plumage, its voice forever stilled,—
      All of the wonder
   Gone that ever filled
Its guise with glory. Oh, bird that I have killed,
   How brilliantly you flew
Across my rapturous vision when first I dreamed of you!

Yet I fling my soul on high with new endeavor,
And I ride the world below with a joyful mind.
I shall start a heron soon
In the marsh beneath the moon—
A wondrous silver heron its inner darkness fledges!
      I beat forever
   The fens and the sedges.
The pledge is still the same—for all disastrous pledges,
      All hopes resigned!
My soul still flies above me for the quarry it shall find.

                    WILLIAM ROSE BENÉT

LITTLE BOY BLUE

Eugene Field was born in St. Louis, Missouri. He early became a reporter on the St. Louis *Evening Journal*. Later he was a columnist for the Denver *Tribune* and the Chicago *Daily News*. His poems were written for the newspapers for which he worked. A complete edition of his poems was published in 1910.

The little toy dog is covered with dust,
　But sturdy and stanch he stands;
The little toy soldier is red with rust,
　And his musket moulds in his hands.
Time was when the little toy dog was new,
　And the soldier was passing fair;
And that was the time when our Little Boy Blue
　Kissed them and put them there.

"Now don't you go till I come," he said,
　"And don't you make any noise!"
So, toddling off to his trundle bed,
　He dreamt of his pretty toys;
And, as he was dreaming, an angel song
　Awakened our Little Boy Blue—
Oh, the years are many, the years are long,
　But the little toy friends are true!

Ay, faithful to Little Boy Blue they stand,
　Each in the same old place,
Awaiting the touch of a little hand,
　The smile of a little face;
And they wonder, as waiting the long years through
　In the dust of that little chair,
What has become of our Little Boy Blue
　Since he kissed and put them there.

EUGENE FIELD

STUPIDITY STREET

Ralph Hodgson is an Englishman who has spent part of his life in America. He loves animals, is an authority on bull terriers, and has been editor, draughtsman, and pressman. He is the author of several small volumes of verse. His most famous poem is "Stupidity Street."

"Stupidity Street" is a forceful protest against the destruction of the lovely things of life to meet utilitarian ends, and against the idleness which fails to destroy things truly noxious.

I saw with open eyes
Singing birds sweet
Sold in the shops
For the people to eat,
Sold in the shops of
Stupidity Street

I saw in vision
The worm in the wheat,
And in the shops nothing
For people to eat;
Nothing for sale in
Stupidity Street.

RALPH HODGSON

MUSIC I HEARD

Conrad Aiken was born in Savannah, Georgia. He was educated at Harvard and by travel. He lives at South Yarmouth, Massachusetts.

Music I heard with you was more than music,
And bread I broke with you was more than bread.
Now that I am without you, all is desolate;
All that was once so beautiful is dead.

Your hands once touched this table and this silver,
And I have seen your fingers hold this glass.
These things do not remember you, belovèd,—
And yet your touch upon them will not pass.

For it was in my heart you moved among them,
And blessed them with your hands and with your eyes;
And in my heart they will remember always,—
They know you once, O beautiful and wise.

CONRAD AIKEN

SONG OF THE FULL CATCH

Constance Lindsay Skinner is an American poet who spent her childhood at a Hudson Bay post. She has always been a student of Indian lore and Indian music. She now lives in New York.

The "Song of the Full Catch" is one of a number of Indian interpretations by Miss Skinner. She says of herself: "My young environment was a Hudson Bay Company's trading-post in Northern British Columbia, and, later, the west coast with its rainy winds and its low-drooping, dragging-boughed cedars—which have sent a lot of long, swishing 's's' into my poems. Now, these Nature Rhythms, as I have named them, are native to us, ours. . . . Only the Indians had composed verse in rhythms drawn from Nature—the advance of light and shadow, the sounds of the winds, waves, brooks, the movements of herds, and the like." The cadences of this poem are very lovely and the language suggests the directness and simplicity of the Indian.

Here's good wind, here's sweet wind,
Here's good wind and my woman calls me!
Straight she stands there by the pine-tree,
Faithful waits she by the cedar,
She will smile and reach her hands
When she sees my thousand salmon!
Here's good wind and my woman calls me.

Here's clear water, here's swift water,
Here's bright water and my woman waits me!
She will call me from the sea's mouth—
Sweet her pine-bed when the morning
Lights my canoe and the river ends!
Here's good wind, here's swift water,
Strong as love when my woman calls me!

CONSTANCE LINDSAY SKINNER

THE LION HOUSE

John Hall Wheelock was born at Far Rockaway, New York. He was educated at Harvard and at the universities of Göttingen and Berlin. He has been with Charles Scribner's Sons in New York since 1911. He is the author of several volumes of poetry. Some of his poems are full of vibrant force, others are as mystical as Emerson's.

"The Lion House" has caught the spirit of Blake, who says:

> "A Robin Redbreast in a cage
> Puts all Heaven in a rage."

How much more dreadful to contemplate is the caged but untamed spirit of the jungle. The diction is admirable and the whole effect is haunting.

> Always the heavy air,
>   The dreadful cage, the low
> Murmur of voices, where
>   Some force goes to and fro
> In an immense despair.
>
> As through a haunted brain,
>   With tireless footfalls
> The Obsession moves again,
>   Trying the floor, the walls,
> Forever, but in vain.
>
> In vain, proud Force! A might,
>   Shrewder than yours, did spin
> Around your rage that bright
>   Prison of steel, wherein
> You pace for my delight.

And oh, my heart, what Doom,
   What warier Will has wrought
The cage, within whose room
   Paces your burning thought—
For the delight of Whom?

JOHN HALL WHEELOCK

A PRAYER FOR A LITTLE HOME

Florence Bone, an English writer, lives at Ripon, Yorkshire. She is the author of historical tales for young people and fairy stories for children. Some of her books are "Dr. Ogilvie's Guest," "The Sapphire Button," and "The Rose-Coloured Wish." She has also written charming poems which have appeared in the London *Spectator* and other periodicals.

"A Prayer for a Little Home" is an illustration of what suggestion can do. In sixteen lines the poem creates for us an ideal home and its environment. Its theme is of universal appeal. The author writes: "I never cease to be amazed at the widespread interest in those verses of mine. I made them one day as I was walking down a Yorkshire lane, and was very bothered about where to find a house. I sent them to *The Spectator*, and have heard of them from all over the world."

God send us a little home
To come back to when we roam—
Low walls and fluted tiles,
Wide windows, a view for miles;
Red firelight and deep chairs;
Small white beds upstairs;
Great talk in little nooks;
Dim colors, rows of books;
One picture on each wall;
Not many things at all.
God send us a little ground—
Tall trees standing round,
Homely flowers in brown sod,
Overhead, Thy stars, O God!
God bless, when winds blow,
Our home and all we know.

FLORENCE BONE

OUR LITTLE HOUSE

Thomas Walsh was born in Brooklyn. He was educated a
Georgetown University and at Columbia. He is an authority
on Spanish literature. He is a contributor to English and Ameri
can magazines and the author of several volumes of poetry.

Our little house upon the hill
In winter-time is strangely still;
The roof-tree, bare of leaves, stands high,
A candelabrum for the sky,
And down below the lamplights glow,
And ours makes answer o'er the snow.

Our little house upon the hill
In summer-time strange voices fill;
With careless rustle of the leaves,
And birds that twitter in the eaves,
And all the vines entangled so
The village lights no longer show.

Our little house upon the hill
Is just the house of Jack and Jill.
And whether showing or unseen,
Hid behind its leafy screen;
There's a star that points it out
When the lamplights are in doubt.

THOMAS WALSH

THE HOUSE ON THE HILL

Edwin Arlington Robinson was born at Head Tide, Maine. He was educated at Gardiner, Maine, and at Harvard. For five years he was in the New York Customs House, but he now devotes himself entirely to the writing of poetry, of which he has published several volumes. He is a member of the National Institute of Arts and Letters.

"The House on the Hill" tries to communicate to others the writer's own reactions toward things and people. Old houses, for instance, affect people differently. To Charles Hanson Towne

> "They are old folk who nod by the fire,
>   Glad with their dreams of youth and desire."

they are mysterious but lovable. On the other hand, "The House on the Hill" inspires a different mood in Edwin Arlington Robinson. He is fascinated by its ruin and decay and the mysteries of lives that have gone away from it. But the result is a sombre poem. The two poems are also very different in pattern and diction. "Old Houses" is conventional in form and wording; "The House on the Hill" is modelled after a difficult French form, the villanelle, which is intricate in pattern and austere in wording.

> They are all gone away,
> The House is shut and still,
> There is nothing more to say.
>
> Through broken walls and gray
> The winds blow bleak and shrill;
> They are all gone away.
>
> Nor is there one to-day
> To speak them good or ill;
> There is nothing more to say.

Why is it then we stray
Around that sunken sill?
They are all gone away.

And our poor fancy-play
For them is wasted skill:
There is nothing more to say.

There is ruin and decay
In the House on the Hill:
They are all gone away;
There is nothing more to say.

EDWIN ARLINGTON ROBINSON

MENDING WALL

For Robert Frost's biography, see "Birches."

Life and labor may be seen from a car as it passes fields where farmers plough and build fences, or founderies where men, stripped to the skin, feed dragon furnaces. But poems interpreting the farmer and the stoker are seldom convincing unless they have been written by men who have ploughed, built fences, or fed furnaces. "Mending Wall" was written by one who has helped to build a stone fence as it should be built, a man working on each side of it. Although the poet says little actually descriptive of his neighbor, we recognize the stolid type, a man who believes as his fathers believed, without reasoning why. He has not the imagination to understand the poet, who mischievously insists on knowing why the wall should be built and what the something is "that doesn't love a wall." The language is plain and farmer-like: "He is all pine and I am apple orchard." The people too are plain, the labor is commonplace, but the effect is satisfying poetry.

Something there is that doesn't love a wall,
That sends the frozen ground-swell under it,
And spills the upper boulders in the sun;
And makes gaps even two can pass abreast.
The work of hunters is another thing:
I have come after them and made repair
Where they have left not one stone on stone,
But they would have the rabbit out of hiding,
To please the yelping dogs. The gaps I mean,
No one has seen them made or heard them made,
But at spring mending-time we find them there.
I let my neighbor know beyond the hill;
And on a day we meet to walk the line
And set the wall between us once again.
We keep the wall between us as we go.
To each the boulders that have fallen to each.

And some are loaves and some so nearly balls
We have to use a spell to make them balance:
"Stay where you are until our backs are turned!"
We wear our fingers rough with handling them.
Oh, just another kind of outdoor game,
One on a side. It comes to little more:
There where it is we do not need the wall:
He is all pine and I am apple orchard.
My apple trees will never get across
And eat the cones under his pines, I tell him.
He only says, "Good fences make good neighbors."
Spring is the mischief in me, and I wonder
If I could put a notion in his head:
"Why do they make good neighbors? Isn't it
Where there are cows? But here there are no cows.
Before I built a wall I'd ask to know
What I was walling in or walling out,
And to whom I was like to give offense.
Something there is that doesn't love a wall,
That wants it down." I could say "Elves" to him,
But it's not elves exactly, and I'd rather
He said it for himself. I see him there
Bringing a stone grasped firmly by the top
In each hand, like an old stone savage armed.
He moves in darkness as it seems to me,
Not of woods only and the shade of trees.
He will not go behind his father's saying,
And he likes having thought of it so well
He says again, "Good fences make good neighbors."

ROBERT FROST

THE HERD BOY

Haniel Long was born at Rangoon, Burmah. He was educated at Exeter and at Harvard. He is associate professor of English in the School of Fine Art, the Carnegie Institute, Pittsburgh. He has published a volume of poetry and is a contributor to current magazines.

"The Herd Boy" recalls the Greek world of beauty; a beauty so keenly felt that it demands immediate and joyous worship. The diction is perfect; no word can be spared.

The night I brought the cows home
   Blue mist was in the air,
And in my heart was heaven
   And on my lips a prayer.

I raised my arms above me,
   I stretched them wide apart,
And all the world was pressing
   In beauty on my heart.

The lane led by a river
   Along an ancient wood,
And ancient thoughts came softly
   As with the leaves they should.

I hung the cows with garlands,
   And proud they walked before;
While mother-naked after
   A laurel branch I bore.

                        HANIEL LONG

THE MOST-SACRED MOUNTAIN

Eunice Tietjens (Mrs. Cloyd Head) was born in Chicago. She has published several volumes of poetry and a novel, and has been associate editor of *Poetry, A Magazine of Verse*. She has studied much abroad. In 1917 she was war correspondent in France for the Chicago *Daily News*.

"The Most-Sacred Mountain" begins with a sharp intake of the breath and a moment of rapture induced by

"Space, and the twelve clean winds of heaven."

As the emotion subsides a little, the rhythm changes and undulates more gently in long lines. Chinese art is suggested in "the slow curves" and "the one black bird" that "circles above the void."

Space, and the twelve clean winds of heaven,
And this sharp exultation, like a cry, after the slow six thou
    sand feet of climbing!
This is Tai Shan, the beautiful, the most holy.

Below my feet the foot-hills nestle, brown with flecks of
    green; and lower down the flat brown plain, the floor of
    earth, stretches away to blue infinity.
Beside me in this airy space the temple roofs cut their slow
    curves against the sky,
And one black bird circles above the void.

Space, and the twelve clean winds are here;
And with them broods eternity—a swift, white peace, a
    presence manifest.
The rhythm ceases here.   Time has no place.
  This is the end that has no end.

Here when Confucius came, a half a thousand years before
    the Nazarene, he stepped with me, thus into timelessness.
The stone beside us waxes old, the carven stone that says:
    On this spot once Confucius stood and felt the smallness of
    the world below.

The stone grows old.
Eternity
Is not for stones.

But I shall go down from this airy space, this swift white
    peace, this stinging exultation;
And time will close about me, and my soul stir to the rhythm
    of the daily round.
Yet, having known, life will not press so close, and always I
    shall feel time ravel thin about me;
For once I stood
In the white windy presence of eternity.

                      EUNICE TIETJENS

PATTERNS

For the biographical sketch of Amy Lowell, see "A Lady."

"Patterns" is often cited as an illustration of what can be done with rhythm in producing new designs. As Marguerite Wilkinson points out in her admirable anthology, "New Voices," the poem is designed in cadences, of which the line "In my stiff brocaded gown" is typical. By repeating this cadence, sometimes with slight alterations, the pattern is made. Some of the reiterated cadences are these:

> "Makes a pink and silver stain."
> "Underneath my stiffened gown."
> "With the weight of this brocade."

The stiffness of the gown, the marked design of the brocade, the formal garden paths—all emphasize the pattern and symbolize the conventional life of the eighteenth century, a life which the woman must lead but from which she longs to escape. Even her grief when she hears that her lover is dead must be as restrained and decorous as her gown and her environment; therefore she orders refreshments for the messenger. Men too are involved in a pattern called war, from which there is no escape. These restrictions are contrasted with the freedom of the daffodils and squills which

> "Flutter in the breeze
> As they please."

The pattern is also reinforced by the colors which run in pairs —pink and silver, blue and yellow.

> I walk down the garden paths,
> And all the daffodils
> Are blowing, and the bright blue squills.
> I walk down the patterned garden paths
> In my stiff, brocaded gown.
> With my powdered hair and jewelled fan,
> I too am a rare
> Pattern. As I wander down
> The garden paths.

My dress is richly figured,
And the train
Makes a pink and silver stain
On the gravel, and the thrift
Of the borders.
Just a plate of current fashion,
Tripping by in high-heeled, ribboned shoes.
Not a softness anywhere about me,
Only whalebone and brocade.
And I sink on a seat in the shade
Of a lime tree. For my passion
Wars against the stiff brocade.
The daffodils and squills
Flutter in the breeze
As they please.
And I weep;
For the lime tree is in blossom
And one small flower has dropped upon my bosom.

And the plashing of waterdrops
In the marble fountain
Comes down the garden paths.
The dripping never stops.
Underneath my stiffened gown
Is the softness of a woman bathing in a marble basin,
A basin in the midst of hedges grown
So thick, she cannot see her lover hiding,
But she guesses he is near,
And the sliding of the water
Seems the stroking of a dear
Hand upon her.
What is Summer in a fine brocaded gown!
I should like to see it lying in a heap upon the ground.
All the pink and silver crumpled up on the ground.

I would be the pink and silver as I ran along the paths,
And he would stumble after,
Bewildered by my laughter.
I should see the sun flashing from his sword-hilt and the
    buckles on his shoes.
I would choose
To lead him in a maze along the patterned paths,
A bright and laughing maze for my heavy-booted lover,
Till he caught me in the shade,
And the buttons of his waistcoat bruised my body as he
    clasped me,
Aching, melting, unafraid.
With the shadows of the leaves and the sundrops,
And the plopping of the waterdrops,
All about us in the open afternoon—
I am very like to swoon
With the weight of this brocade,
For the sun sifts through the shade.

Underneath the fallen blossom
In my bosom,
Is a letter I have hid.
It was brought to me this morning by a rider from the Duke.
"Madam, we regret to inform you that Lord Hartwell
Died in action Thursday se'nnight."
As I read it in the white, morning sunlight,
The letters squirmed like snakes.
"Any answer, Madam?" said my footman.
"No," I told him.
"See that the messenger takes some refreshment.
No, no answer."
And I walked into the garden,
Up and down the patterned paths,

In my stiff, correct brocade.
The blue and yellow flowers stood up proudly in the sun,
Each one.
I stood upright too,
Held rigid to the pattern
By the stiffness of my gown.
Up and down I walked,
Up and down.

In a month he would have been my husband.
In a month, here, underneath this lime,
We would have broke the pattern;
He for me, and I for him,
He as Colonel, I as Lady,
On this shady seat.
He had a whim
That sunlight carried blessing.
And I answered, "It shall be as you have said."
Now he is dead.

In Summer and in Winter I shall walk
Up and down
The patterned garden paths
In my stiff, brocaded gown.
The squills and daffodils
Will give place to pillared roses, and to asters, and to snow.
I shall go
Up and down,
In my gown.
Gorgeously arrayed,
Boned and stayed.
And the softness of my body will be guarded from embrace
By each button, hook, and lace.

For the man who should loose me is dead,
Fighting with the Duke of Flanders
In a pattern called a war.
Christ! What are patterns for?

AMY LOWELL

AMERICA

AMERICA THE BEAUTIFUL

For the biographical sketch of Katharine Lee Bates, see "Yellow Warblers."

"America the Beautiful" is the official hymn of the American Federation of Women's Clubs. In its treatment there is a spaciousness which is suited to the vast expanse of our country and to the great deeds of pioneering and of liberating warfare. The poem is also a prayer for the fulfilment of America's mission, the crowning of her good with brotherhood.

O beautiful for spacious skies,
 For amber waves of grain,
For purple mountain majesties
 Above the fruited plain!
  America! America!
 God shed His grace on thee
And crown thy good with brotherhood
 From sea to shining sea!

O beautiful for pilgrim feet,
 Whose stern, impassioned stress
A thoroughfare for freedom beat
 Across the wilderness!
  America! America!
 God mend thine every flaw,
Confirm thy soul in self-control,
 Thy liberty in law!

O beautiful for heroes proved
 In liberating strife,
Who more than self their country loved,
 And mercy more than life!
  America! America!

May God thy gold refine
Till all success be nobleness
And every gain divine!

O beautiful for patriot dream
That sees beyond the years
Thine alabaster cities gleam
Undimmed by human tears!
America! America!
God shed His grace on thee
And crown thy good with brotherhood
From sea to shining sea!

KATHARINE LEE BATES

ARIZONA
The Windmills

For the biographical sketch of John Gould Fletcher, see
'Spring.''
"The Windmills" is an illustration of the methods of the
Imagists: the use of the exact word, a rhythm that is suited to
the theme, exact particulars. Color, heat, dust, and metallic
sounds are so faithfully expressed that when we have read the
poem we have been in Arizona. Furthermore, we have shared
the mood of the writer.

The windmills, like great sunflowers of steel,
Lift themselves proudly over the straggling houses;
And at their feet the deep blue-green alfalfa
Cuts the desert like the stroke of a sword.

Yellow melon flowers
Crawl beneath the withered peach-trees;
A date-palm throws its heavy fronds of steel
Against the scoured metallic sky.

The houses, double-roofed for coolness,
Cower amid the manzanita scrub.
A man with jingling spurs
Walks heavily out of a vine-bowered doorway,
Mounts his pony, rides away.

The windmills stare at the sun.
The yellow earth cracks and blisters.
Everything is still.

In the afternoon
The wind takes dry waves of heat and tosses them,

Mingled with dust, up and down the streets,
Against the belfry with its green bells:

And, after sunset, when the sky
Becomes a green and orange fan,
The windmills, like great sunflowers on dried stalks,
Stare hard at the sun they cannot follow.

Turning, turning, forever turning
In the chill night-wind that sweeps over the valley,
With the shriek and the clank of the pumps groaning be-
neath them,
And the choking gurgle of tepid water.

JOHN GOULD FLETCHER

VIRGINIANA

Mary Johnston was born at Buchanan, Virginia, and educated at home. She is the author of many novels of distinguished quality, the most famous of which is "To Have and to Hold." She lives at "Three Hills," Warm Springs, Virginia.

Slow turns the water by the green marshes,
In Virginia.
Overhead the sea fowl
Make silver flashes, cry harsh as peacocks.
Capes and islands stand,
Ocean thunders,
The lighthouses burn red and gold stars.
In Virginia
Run a hundred rivers.
The dogwood is in blossom,
The pink honeysuckle,
The fringe tree.
My love is the ghostly armed sycamore,
My loves are the yellow pine and the white pine,
My love is the mountain linden,
Mine is the cedar.

Ancient forest,
Hemlock-mantled cliff,
Black cohosh,
Goldenrod, ironweed,
And purple farewell-summer,
Maple red in the autumn,
And plunge of the mountain brook.

The wind bends the wheat ears,
The wind bends the corn,
The wild grape to the vineyard grape
Sends the season's greetings.
Timothy, clover,
Apple, peach!
The blue grass talks to the moss and fern.

Sapphire-shadowed, deep-bosomed, long-limbed,
Mountains lie in the garden of the sky,
Evening is a passion flower, morning is a rose!
Old England sailed to Virginia,
Bold Scotland sailed,
Vine-wreathed France sailed,
And the Rhine sailed,
And Ulster and Cork and Killarney.
Out of Africa—out of Africa!
Guinea Coast, Guinea Coast,
Senegambia, Dahomey—
Now one,
In Virginia.

Pocahontas steals through the forest,
Along the Blue Ridge ride the Knights of the Horseshoe,
Young George Washington measures neighbor's land from
    neighbor,
In the firelight Thomas Jefferson plays his violin,
Violin, violin!
Patrick Henry speaks loud in Saint John's church,
Andrew Lewis lifts his flintlock.—
O Fringed Hunting Shirt, where are you going?
George Rogers Clark takes Kaskaskia and Vincennes.

They tend tobacco
And they hoe corn,
Colored folk singing,
Singing sweetly of heaven
And the Lord Jesus.
Broad are the tobacco leaves,
Narrow are the corn blades,
Little blue morning-glories run through the corn fields.

Sumach, sumach!
Blue-berried cedar,
Persimmon and pawpaw,
Chinquepin.
Have you seen the 'possum?
Have you seen the 'coon?
Have you heard the whippoorwill?
Whippoorwill! Whippoorwill!
Whip-poor-will!

White-top wagons
Rolling westward.
Bearded men
Looking westward.
Women, children,
Gazing westward.
Kentucky!
Ohio!
Halt at eve and build the fire.
Dogs,
Long guns,
Household gear.
'Ware the Indians!
White-top wagons going westward.

Edgar Allan Poe
Walking in the moonlight,
In the woods of Albemarle,
'Neath the trees of Richmond,
Pondering names of women,
Annabel—Annie,
Lenore—Ulalume.

Maury, Maury!
What of Winds and Currents?
Maury, Maury,
Ocean rover!
But when you come to die,
"Carry me through Goshen Pass
When the rhododendron is in bloom!"

Men in gray,
Men in blue,
Very young men,
Meet by a river.
Overhead are fruit trees.
Water—water!
"We will drink, then fight."—
"O God, why do we
Fight anyhow?
It's a good swimming-hole
And the cherries are ripe!"
Bronze men on bronze horses,
Down the long avenue,
They ride in the sky,
Bronze men.
Stuart cries to Jackson,
Jackson cries to Lee,

Lee to Washington.
Bronze men,
Great soldiers.

The church bells ring,
In Virginia.
Sonorous,
Sweet,
In the sunshine,
In the rain.

Salvation! It is Sunday,
Salvation! It is Sunday,
In Virginia.
Locust trees in bloom,
Long grass in the churchyard,
June bugs zooning round the roses,
First bell, second bell!
All the ladies are in church,
Now the men will follow,
In Virginia,
In Virginia.

MARY JOHNSTON

ON THE GREAT PLATEAU

Edith Wyatt was born in Wisconsin. She is a graduate of
Bryn Mawr. She has written much both in prose and verse.
Her home is in Chicago.

To one who loves the West a distant horizon is necessary.
One must have space in which to be happy. "On the Great
Plateau" interprets this feeling. The scale of things is immense:
great open spaces, great distances, lofty mountains, deep valleys.
The rhythm suits the theme: "Far and far away—far away."

In the Santa Clara Valley, far away and far away,
Cool-breathed waters dip and dally, linger towards another
    day—
Far and far away—far away.

Slow their floating step, but tireless, terraced down the great
    Plateau.
Towards our ways of steam and wireless, silver-paced the
    brook-beds go.
Past the ladder-walled Pueblos, past the orchards, pear and
    quince,
Where the back-locked river's ebb flows, miles and miles the
    valley glints,
Shining backwards, singing downwards, towards horizons
    blue and bay.
All the roofs the roads ensconce so dream of visions far
    away—
Santa Cruz and Ildefonso, Santa Clara, Santa Fé.
Ancient, sacred fears and faiths, ancient, sacred faiths and
    fears—
Some were real, some were wraiths—Indian, Franciscan years
Built the Khivas, swung the bells; while the wind sang plain
    and free,

'Turn your eyes from visioned hells!—look as far as you can
    see!"
In the Santa Clara Valley, far away and far away,
Dying dreams divide and dally, crystal-terraced waters
    sally—
Linger towards another day, far and far away—far away.

As you follow where you find them, up along the high Plateau,
In the hollows left behind them Spanish chapels fade be-
    low—
Shaded court and low corrals. In the vale the goat-herd
    browses.
Hollyhocks are seneschals by the little buff-walled houses.
Over grassy swale and alley have you ever seen it so—
Up the Santa Clara Valley, riding on the Great Plateau?
Past the ladder-walled Pueblos, past the orchards, pear and
    quince,
Where the trenchèd waters' ebb flows, miles and miles the
    valley glints,
Shining backwards, singing downwards towards horizons blue
    and bay.
All the haunts the bluffs ensconce so breathe of visions far
    away,
As you ride near Ildefonso back again to Santa Fé.
Pecos, mellow with the years, tall-walled Taos—who can
    know
Half the storied faiths and fears haunting green New Mexico?
Only from her open places down arroyos blue and bay,
One wild grace of many graces dallies towards another day.
Where her yellow tufa crumbles, something stars and grasses
    know,
Something true, that crowns and humbles, shimmers from
    the Great Plateau:

Blows where cool-paced waters dally from the stillness of
Puyé,
Down the Santa Clara Valley through the world from far
away—
Far and far away—far away.

EDITH WYATT

GHOSTS OF THE NEW WORLD
"There are no ghosts in America"

The biographical sketch of Alfred Noyes will be found in connection with "Princeton."

There are no ghosts, you say,
To haunt her blaze of light;
No shadows in her day,
No phantoms in her night.
Columbus' tattered sail
Has passed beyond our hail.

What? On that magic coast,
Where Raleigh fought with fate,
Or where the Devon ghost
Unbarred the Golden Gate,
No dark, strange, earringed men
Beat in from sea again?

No ghosts in Salem town
With silver-buckled shoon?
No lovely witch to drown
Or burn beneath the moon?
Not even a whiff of tea
On Boston's glimmering quay?

O, ghostly Spanish walls,
Where brown Franciscans glide,
Is there no voice that calls
Across the Great Divide,
To pilgrims on their way
Along the Santa Fé?

Then let your Pullman cars
Go roaring to the West,
Till, watched by lonelier stars,
The cactus lifts its crest.
There, on that painted plain,
One ghost will rise again.

Majestic and forlorn,
Wreck of a dying race,
The Red Man, half in scorn,
Shall raise his haughty face,
Inscrutable as the sky,
To watch our ghosts go by.

What? Is earth dreaming still?
Shall not the night disgorge
The ghosts of Bunker Hill,
The ghosts of Valley Forge,
Or, England's mightiest son,
The ghost of Washington?

No ghosts where Lincoln fell?
No ghosts for seeing eyes?
I know an old cracked bell
Shall make a million rise
When one immortal ghost
Calls on the slumbering host.

                              ALFRED NOYES

LABOR AND DEMOCRACY

WORK

Henry van Dyke is an American, the author of many volumes of verse, essays, and short stories. He was born in Pennsylvania and educated at Princeton and other universities. He was professor of English at Princeton for many years. For three years he was United States Minister to the Netherlands.

Let me but do my work from day to day,
In field or forest, at the desk or loom,
In roaring market-place or tranquil room;
Let me but find it in my heart to say,
When vagrant wishes beckon me astray,
"This is my work; my blessing, not my doom;
Of all who live, I am the one by whom
This work can best be done in the right way."

Then shall I see it not too great, nor small,
To suit my spirit and to prove my powers;
Then shall I cheerful greet the laboring hours,
And cheerful turn, when the long shadows fall
At eventide, to play and love and rest,
Because I know for me my work is best.

HENRY VAN DYKE

CARGOES

For the biographical sketch of John Masefield, see "Sea-Fever."

As set forth elsewhere in this book, certain poets reveal their ideas best through symbols. "Cargoes" is an illustration of the use of symbols. Commerce is pictured in three widely separated periods; approximately in the time of King Solomon, in the days of Queen Elizabeth, and in our own time. But "Cargoes" is more than three pictures. It is a revelation of world-conditions both moral and spiritual. Some feel a sense of anticlimax in reading the last stanza. "Why end with anything so ugly?" they ask. If it is ugly, it is necessary ugliness. The "dirty British coaster" is a better thing than the quinquireme and the galleon with their unseen groaning, hopeless slaves. And the coaster's cargo means more comfort to the world than do the tropical luxuries carried by the ships of Nineveh and Spain.

"Cargoes" works enchantment on the reader by its color and its rhythms "of the many-bubbled brine" as the sea is mastered in turn by oars, by sails, and by steam.

Quinquireme of Nineveh from distant Ophir,
Rowing home to haven in sunny Palestine,
    With a cargo of ivory
    And apes and peacocks,
Sandalwood, cedarwood, and sweet, white wine.

Stately Spanish galleon coming from the Isthmus,
Dipping through the Tropics by the palm-green shores
    With a cargo of diamonds,
    Emeralds, amethysts,
Topazes, and cinnamon, and gold moidores.

Dirty British coaster with a salt-caked smoke stack,
Butting through the channel in the mad March days
    With a cargo of Tyne coal,
    Road rails, pig lead,
Firewood, ironware, and cheap tin trays.

JOHN MASEFIELD

CALIBAN IN THE COAL MINES

Louis Untermeyer is a successful wholesale jeweler, an editor of anthologies, one of the foremost living critics, and a poet of importance. He was born in New York City and educated at the De Witt Clinton High School. His wife, Jean Starr Untermeyer, is also a poet. They live in New York.

"Caliban in the Coal Mines" should be compared with "The Miner," by Richard Burton. In Mr. Burton's poem is warm human sympathy with labor. In Mr. Untermeyer's poem the writer identifies himself with the miner who prays for a "handful of stars" to light the blackness and the dangers of his place of toil.

God, we don't like to complain—
    We know that the mine is no lark—
But—there's the pools from the rain;
    But—there's the cold and the dark.

God, You don't know what it is—
    You, in Your well-lighted sky,
Watching the meteors whizz;
    Warm, with the sun always by.

God, if You had but the moon
    Stuck in Your cap for a lamp,
Even You'd tire of it soon,
    Down in the dark and the damp.

Nothing but blackness above,
    And nothing that moves but the cars—
God, if You wish for our love,
    Fling us a handful of stars!

                    LOUIS UNTERMEYER

THE MINER

Richard Burton was born at Hartford, Connecticut. He received his A.B. from Trinity College, Connecticut, and his Ph.D. from Johns Hopkins. He was for a number of years the head of the English Department of the University of Minnesota. He has done much very important editorial work. He has written criticism, essays, fiction, and drama. He is a member of the National Institute of Arts and Letters and has been president of the Drama League of America.

Up creaks the car; he leaves his ghastly dream
Of flickering, strange lights and caverns gloomed,
Grim fears of death-damp and the rumblings deep
Of an inferno whence the damned come back
Daily to taste of Paradise, before
The Devil bids them down; up creaks the car
Disgorging men and mud indifferently.

How sweet the lingering sun, and yonder, look,
The cabin lights are beckoning fondly, where
Warm love awaits him; for a little space
He's no machine but human, and his God
Our God,—no mid-earth Devil, but a power
Benign and near. . . .
                    But now the nether pit
Reclaims these children of a double world,
And once again Life is a nightmare dream.

                                        RICHARD BURTON

THE MAN WITH THE HOE

Written after seeing Millet's world-famous painting

For the biographical sketch of Edwin Markham, see "Lincoln." "The Man with the Hoe" dates back to 1899. Its protest against social injustice was so flaming that the world was startled. The poem was quoted by the press everywhere and called "the battle-cry of the next thousand years." With Millet's famous painting as his text, the author has pictured the hopeless and ignorant man enslaved by toil, and has foretold the menace he will become to civilization.

Bowed by the weight of centuries he leans
Upon his hoe and gazes on the ground,
The emptiness of ages in his face,
And on his back the burden of the world.
Who made him dead to rapture and despair,
A thing that grieves not and that never hopes,
Stolid and stunned, a brother to the ox?
Who loosened and let down this brutal jaw?
Whose was the hand that slanted back this brow?
Whose breath blew out the light within this brain?

Is this the Thing the Lord God made and gave
To have dominion over sea and land;
To trace the stars and search the heavens for power;
To feel the passion of Eternity?
Is this the dream He dreamed who shaped the suns
And marked their ways upon the ancient deep?
Down all the caverns of Hell to their last gulf
There is no shape more terrible than this—
More tongued with censure of the world's blind greed—
More filled with signs and portents for the soul—
More packt with danger to the universe.

What gulfs between him and the seraphim!
Slave of the wheel of labor, what to him
Are Plato and the swing of Pleiades?
What the long reaches of the peaks of song,
The rift of dawn, the reddening of the rose?
Through this dread shape the suffering ages look;
Time's tragedy is in that aching stoop;
Through this dread shape humanity betrayed,
Plundered, profaned and disinherited,
Cries protest to the Judges of the World,
A protest that is also prophecy.

O masters, lords and rulers in all lands,
Is this the handiwork you give to God,
This monstrous thing, distorted and soul-quenched?
How will you ever straighten up this shape;
Touch it again with immortality;
Give back the upward looking and the light;
Rebuild in it the music and the dream;
Make right the immemorial infamies,
Perfidious wrongs, immedicable woes?

O masters, lords and rulers in all lands,
How will the future reckon with this man?
How answer his brute question in that hour
When whirlwinds of rebellion shake the world?
How will it be with kingdoms and with kings—
With those who shaped him to the thing he is—
When this dumb terror shall appeal to God,
After the silence of the centuries?

EDWIN MARKHAM

THE EXCAVATION

Clusters of electric bulbs
Like giant chrysanthemums
Paint the black cavern
With streaks and blots
Of faded yellow.
In grotesque mimicry
The monstrous shadows
Ape each movement of toiling men.

The stale pungent odor of unpacked earth
Tickles the nostrils.
Through the wood-plank roof
The dull-booming rumble
Of scampering traffic
Trickles in—
But is swallowed up
By the harsh purr of the drill
As it bites frenziedly
Into the dogged rock.

Overhead, unseen,
A mountain of stone is kept upright
By a slender steel beam
And a theory.

MAX ENDICOFF

CENTRAL

John Curtis Underwood lives in Santa Fé, New Mexico. He has published four volumes of poetry and done much editorial and magazine work.

Though men may build their bridges high and plant their
    piers below the sea,
And drive their trains across the sky, a higher task is left to
    me.
I bridge the void 'twixt soul and soul; I bring the longing
    lovers near.
I draw you to your spirit's goal. I serve the ends of fraud
    and fear.

The older fates sat in the sun. The cords they spun were
    short and slight.
I set my stitches one by one, where life electric fetters night
Till it outstrips the planet's speed, and out of darkness leaps
    to-day;
And men in Maine shall hear and heed a voice from San
    Francisco Bay.

JOHN CURTIS UNDERWOOD

WOOLWORTH TOWER

For the biographical sketch of William Rose Benét, see "The Falconer of God."

"Woolworth Tower," a fragment from "The Singing Sky-scrapers," has a charm of its own, although the theme and the treatment are daring and unusual. Of it Louis Untermeyer says, "In the voices of the titanic buildings calling each other across the night, we have a new sort of mysticism—one that with its blend of splendor and stridency is wholly American."

And far to the South
I heard the Woolworth Tower
Reply from the sky:

"Aye, cities of power,
Each a granite flower
Stamened to unfold
With towers of ivory,
Towers of gold,
Towers of brass
And towers of iron
Towers as many as the hours that environ
The years of our servitude,
Our steel and iron yoke.
In the deep blue skies
They stand like smoke!
Pavia the hundred-towered,
Shining over Italy,
The Greek Heliopolis,
The City of the Sun—
Phœnician Sidon,
Persian Persepolis,
The Vale of Siddim's cities

By sins undone!
There the strong rampires
Of Troy flare fires.
There like spears stand spires.
Priceless citadels
Pulsate with their pæan
Æon after æon:
'We are the eternal,
Your frame but shells!
We are your sires,
The frozen fierce desires
Of Man made immortal
By temple-miracles.'"

WILLIAM ROSE BENÉT

GOETHALS, THE PROPHET–ENGINEER

Percy Mackaye is an American poet, lecturer, and dramatist. He was educated at Harvard and Leipsic. He directs many of his own masques. A number of his plays have been successfully produced on the professional stage. He is a member of the National Institute of Arts and Letters.

"Goethals, the Prophet-Engineer," was read by the author at the presentation to Goethals of the Civic Forum medal by John H. Finley, head of the New York educational system. It is characteristic of to-day that a poet should have considered an engineering feat worth a song of triumph. The swing of the lines, the diction, the pictures—all are in harmony with the theme. We hear the giant machinery ring in dithyrambs in its contest with mountains and seas.

A man went down to Panama
Where many a man had died
To slit the sliding mountains
And lift the Eternal tide:
A man stood up in Panama,
And the mountains stood aside.

For a poet wrought in Panama
With a continent for his theme,
And he wrote with flood and fire
To forge a planet's dream,
And the derricks rang in dithyrambs
And his stanzas roared in steam.

Where old Balboa bent his gaze
He leads the liners through,
And the Horn that tossed Magellan
Bellows a far halloo.
For where the navies never sailed
Steamed Goethals and his crew.

So nevermore the tropic routes
Need poleward warp and veer,
But on through the Gates of Goethals
The steady keels shall steer,
Where the tribes of man are led toward peace
By the prophet-engineer.

PERCY MACKAYE

SATURDAY NIGHT

For the biographical sketch of James Oppenheim, see "The Runner in the Skies."

The lights of Saturday night beat golden, golden over the
pillared street;
The long plate-glass of a Dream-World olden is as the foot-
lights shining sweet.
Street-lamp—flambeau—glamour of trolley—comet-trail of
the trains above,
Splash where the jostling crowds are jolly with echoing laughter and human love.

This is the City of the Enchanted, and these are her enchanted people;
Far and far is Daylight, haunted with whistle of mill and bell
of steeple.
The eastern tenements loose the women, the western flats
release the wives
To touch, where all the ways are common, a glory to their
sweated lives.

The leather of shoes in the brilliant casement sheds a lustre
over the heart;
The high-heaped fruit in the flaring basement glows with the
tints of Turner's art.
Darwin's dream and the eye of Spencer saw not such a gloried
race
As here, in copper light intenser than desert sun, glides face
by face.

This drab washwoman dazed and breathless, ray-chiselled in
    the golden stream,
Is a magic statue standing deathless, her tub and soapsuds
    touched with Dream.
Yea, in this people, glamour-sunnied, democracy wins heaven
    again;
Here the unlearned and the unmoneyed laugh in the lights of
    Lover's Lane!

O Dream-World lights that lift through the ether millions of
    miles to the Milky Way!
To-night earth rolls through a golden weather that lights the
    Pleiades where they play!
Yet—God? Does he lead these sons and daughters? Yea
    do they feel with a passion that stills,
God on the face of the moving waters, God in the quiet of the
    hills?

Yet—what if the million-mantled mountains, and what if the
    million-moving sea
Are here alone in façades and fountains—our deep stone
    world of humanity—
We builders of cities and civilizations, walled away from the
    sea and the sod,
Must reach, dream-led, for our revelations through one
    another—as far as God.

Through one another—through one another—no more the
    gleam on sea or land,
But so close that we see the Brother, and understand—and
    understand!
Till, drawn in swept crowd closer, closer, we see the gleam
    the human clod,
And clerk and foreman, peddler and grocer, are in our Family
    of God!   JAMES OPPENHEIM

THE UNCONQUERED AIR

Florence Earle Coates (née Earle) was born in Philadelphia. She was educated in private schools in America, France, and Belgium. She is a contributor to many of the best-known magazines, and author of several volumes of poetry. She has been elected Poet Laureate of Pennsylvania by the State Federation of Clubs.

Mrs. Coates might have taken for her text, "Thou madest him (man) a little lower than the angels: thou crownedst him with glory and honor, and didst set him over the works of thy hands." The poem in its diction and imagery belongs to an earlier period, but in its theme it belongs to the present.

I

(1906)

Others endure Man's rule: he therefore deems
I shall endure it—I, the unconquered Air!
Imagines this triumphant strength may bear
His paltry sway! yea, ignorantly dreams,
Because proud Rhea now his vassal seems,
And Neptune him obeys in billowy lair,
That he a more sublime assault may dare,
Where blown by tempest wild the vulture screams!
Presumptuous, he mounts: I toss his bones
Back from the height supernal he has braved:
Aye, as his vessel nears my perilous zones,
I blow the cockle-shell away like chaff
And give him to the Sea he has enslaved.
He founders in its depths; and then I laugh!

II

(1911)

Impregnable I held myself, secure
Against intrusion. Who can measure Man?
How should I guess his mortal will outran
Defeat so far that danger could allure
For its own sake?—that he would all endure,
All sacrifice, all suffer, rather than
Forego the daring dreams Olympian
That prophesy to him of victory sure?
Ah, tameless Courage!—dominating power
That, all attempting, in a deathless hour
Made earth-born Titans godlike, in revolt!—
Fear is the fire that melts Icarian wings:
Who fears nor Fate, nor Time, nor what Time brings
May drive Apollo's steeds, or wield the thunderbolt!

FLORENCE EARLE COATES

THE SISTERS

Louise Ayres Garnett (née Ayres) was born at Plymouth, Indiana, and educated at Knickerbacker Hall, Indianapolis, and at Dearborn Seminary, Chicago. She has written several books of poetry and many published songs. She is also the author of several plays with incidental music, and the text for two oratorios by Henry Hadley.

The struggle of the Mary and Martha in every woman is here quaintly and charmingly described, even with a mischievous touch as when Mary one day hides the dust-cloth and broom. The reconciliation of the sisters is one all women devoutly desire.

The Martha-in-me filled her days
With tasks devoid of joy and praise;
She polished well the furniture;
She made the locks and bolts secure;
She trimmed the lamps with barren ease;
She rubbed the ivory of the keys;
She made the windows shine and glow;
She washed the linen fair as snow.

The Mary-in-me did not stay
At home, as Martha did, each day;
She held aloof like some wild bird
Whose music is but seldom heard.
My Martha felt a little shy
Of Mary as she passed her by,
And one day hid the cloth and broom
With which she garnishes my room.

When Mary saw, she paused and pressed
A hand of Martha to her breast,
And whispered, "We must learn to do
Our labors side by side, we two."

So have the sisters found delight
In doing fireside tasks aright;
Together they have come to see
The meaning in mahogany,
Which now they rub that there may pass
A pageant in its looking-glass;
They shine the windows that the bloom
Of earth be brought within my room;
The lamps are gladly filled and trimmed
And virgin wisdom goes undimmed;
They polish the piano keys
In readiness for harmonies;
In bolting doors they've learned as well
To throw them wide for heaven and hell
That all who will may enter there
To be the guests of grace and prayer.

Mary and Martha in sisterhood
Dwell in me as sisters should;
They fashion a garment and kiss its hem,
And my house is in order because of them.

LOUISE AYRES GARNETT

THE COMMON STREET

Helen Gray Cone was born in New York City. She was educated in New York Normal College (now Hunter College), where she has been professor of English since 1899.
"The Common Street" is a poem of beautiful contrasts.

The common street climbed up against the sky,
Gray meeting gray; and wearily to and fro
I saw the patient, common people go,
Each with his sordid burden trudging by.
And the rain dropped; there was not any sigh
Or stir of a live wind; dull, dull and slow
All motion; as a tale told long ago
The faded world; and creeping night drew nigh.

Then burst the sunset, flooding far and fleet,
Leavening the whole of life with magic leaven.
Suddenly down the long wet glistening hill
Pure splendor poured—and lo! the common street,
A golden highway into golden heaven,
With the dark shapes of men ascending still.

HELEN GRAY CONE

PATH FLOWER

Olive Tilford Dargan (née Tilford) was born in Kentucky
She was educated at the University of Nashville and at Radcliff
College. She has published several volumes of poems and plays
"The Cycle's Rim" was awarded the five-hundred-dollar prize
given by the Southern Society of New York for the best book o
the year by a Southern writer. Mrs. Dargan lives in New York
although she spends part of her time among the mountains o
her native State.

"Path Flower" is a poem of human interest. The simple bal
lad form is beautifully adapted to the theme, and both dictio
and imagery have delicate charm.

A redcap sang in Bishop's wood,
    A lark o'er Golder's lane,
As I the April pathway trod
    Bound west for Willesden.

At foot each tiny blade grew big
    And taller stood to hear,
And every leaf on every twig
    Was like a little ear.

As I too paused, and both ways tried
    To catch the rippling rain,—
So still, a hare kept at my side
    His tussock of disdain,—

Behind me close I heard a step,
    A soft pit-pat surprise,
And looking round my eyes fell deep
    Into sweet other eyes;

The eyes like wells, where sun lies too,
  So clear and trustful brown,
Without a bubble warning you
  That here's a place to drown.

"How many miles?" Her broken shoes
  Had told of more than one.
She answered like a dreaming Muse,
  "I came from Islington."

"So long a tramp?" Two gentle nods
  Then seemed to lift a wing,
And words fell soft as willow buds,
  "I came to find the Spring."

A timid voice, yet not afraid
  In ways so sweet to roam,
As it with honey-bees had played
  And could no more go home.

Her home! I saw the human lair,
  I heard the hucksters bawl,
I stifled with the thickened air
  Of bickering mart and stall.

Without a tuppence for a ride,
  Her feet had set her free.
Her rags, that decency defied,
  Seemed new with liberty.

But she was frail. Who would might note
  The trail of hungering

That for an hour she had forgot
  In wonder of the Spring.

So shriven by her joy she glowed
  It seemed a sin to chat.
(A tea-shop snuggled off the road;
  Why did I think of that?)

Oh, frail, so frail! I could have wept,—
  But she was passing on,
And I but muddled, "You'll accept
  A penny for a bun?"

Then up her little throat a spray
  Of rose climbed for it must;
A wilding lost till safe it lay
  Hid by her curls of rust;

And I saw modesties at fence
  With pride that bore no name;
So old it was she knew not whence
  It sudden woke and came;

But that which shone of all most clear
  Was startled, sadder thought
That I should give her back the fear
  Of life she had forgot.

And I blushed for the world we'd made,
  Putting God's hand aside,
Till for the want of sun and shade
  His little children died;

And blushed that I who every year
    With Spring went up and down,
Must greet a soul that ached for her
    With "penny for a bun!"

Struck as a thief in holy place
    Whose sin upon him cries,
I watched the flowers leave her face,
    The song go from her eyes.

Then she, sweet heart, she saw my rout,
    And of her charity
A hand of grace put softly out
    And took the coin from me.

A redcap sang in Bishop's wood,
    A lark o'er Golder's lane;
But I, alone, still glooming stood,
    And April plucked in vain;

Till living words rang in my ears
    And sudden music played:
Out of such sacred thirst as hers
    The world shall be remade.

Afar she turned her head and smiled
    As might have smiled the Spring,
And humble as a wondering child
    I watched her vanishing.

                    OLIVE TILFORD DARGAN

IN LADY STREET

John Drinkwater is an English poet and playwright. He is
the manager of the Birmingham Repertory Theatre. "Abraham
Lincoln" is his best-known play.

All day long the traffic goes
In Lady Street by dingy rows
Of sloven houses, tattered shops—
Fried fish, old clothes and fortune-tellers—
Tall trams on silver-shining rails,
With grinding wheels and swaying tops,
And lorries with their corded bales,
And screeching cars. "Buy, Buy!" the sellers
Of rags and bones and sickening meat
Cry all day long in Lady Street.

And when the sunshine has its way
In Lady Street, then all the gray
Dull desolation grows in state
More dull and gray and desolate,
And the sun is a shamefast thing,
A lord not comely-housed, a god
Seeing what gods must blush to see,
A song where it is ill to sing,
And each gold ray despiteously
Lies like a gold ironic rod.

Yet one gray man in Lady Street
Looks for the sun. He never bent
Life to his will, his travelling feet
Have scaled no cloudy continent,
Nor has the sickle-hand been strong.

He lives in Lady Street; a bed,
Four cobwebbed walls.

But all day long
A time is singing in his head
Of youth in Gloucester lanes. He hears
The wind among the barley-blades,
The tapping of the woodpeckers
On the smooth beeches, thistle-spades
Slicing the sinewy roots; he sees
The hooded filberts in the copse
Beyond the loaded orchard trees,
The netted avenues of hops;
He smells the honeysuckle thrown
Along the hedge. He lives alone,
Alone—yet not alone, for sweet
Are Gloucester lanes in Lady Street.

Aye, Gloucester lanes. For down below
The cobwebbed room this gray man plies
A trade, a colored trade. A show
Of many-colored merchandise
Is in his shop. Brown filberts there,
And apples red with Gloucester air,
And cauliflowers he keeps, and round
Smooth marrows grown on Gloucester ground,
Fat cabbages and yellow plums,
And gaudy brave chrysanthemums.
And times a glossy pheasant lies
Among his store, not Tyrian dyes
More rich than are the neck-feathers;
And times a prize of violets,
Or dewy mushrooms satin-skinned,

And times an unfamiliar wind
Robbed of its woodland flavor stirs
Gay daffodils this gray man sets
Among his treasure.

　　　　　All day long
In Lady Street the traffic goes
By dingy houses, desolate rows
Of shops that stare like hopeless eyes.
Day long the sellers cry their cries,
The fortune-tellers tell no wrong
Of lives that know not any right,
And drift, that has not even the will
To drift, toils through the day until
The wage of sleep is won at night.
But this gray man heeds not at all
The hell of Lady Street. His stall
Of many-colored merchandise
He makes a shining paradise,
As all day long chrysanthemums
He sells, and red and yellow plums
And cauliflowers. In that one spot
Of Lady Street the sun is not
Ashamed to shine and send a rare
Shower of color through the air;
The gray man says the sun is sweet
On Gloucester lanes in Lady Street.

JOHN DRINKWATER

AUTUMN

(*To My Mother*)

Jean Starr Untermeyer (née Starr) was born at Zanesville, Ohio. She is the wife of Louis Untermeyer, a writer mentioned elsewhere in this book. She wrote at first in free verse, but her later work shows definite rhythmical plan. Her poems are published in "Growing Pains" and "Dreams Out of Darkness."

To get the author's idea of her art one should read "Clay Hills." She spares no pains to make her work true. She seeks —and finds—the exact word, and paints pictures of extraordinary vividness. Amy Lowell says of "Autumn," "Verhaeren's Flemish genre pictures are no better." Few have found in the kitchen's activities of pickling and canning an inspiration for poems; but Jean Starr Untermeyer has dignified and justified her choice of subject.

How memory cuts away the years,
And how clean the picture comes
Of autumn days, brisk and busy;
Charged with keen sunshine.
And you, stirred with activity,
The spirit of those energetic days.

There was our back yard,
So plain and stripped of green,
With even the weeds carefully pulled away
From the crooked red bricks that made the walk,
And the earth on either side so black.

Autumn and dead leaves burning in the sharp air.
And winter comforts coming in like a pageant.
I shall not forget them:—
Great jars laden with the raw green of pickles,

Standing in a solemn row across the back of the porch,
Exhaling the pungent dill;
And in the very centre of the yard,
You, tending the great catsup kettle of gleaming copper,
Where fat, red tomatoes bobbed up and down
Like jolly monks in a drunken dance.

And there were bland banks of cabbages that came by the
　　wagon-load,
Soon to be cut into delicate ribbons
Only to be crushed by the heavy, wooden stompers.
Such feathery whiteness—to come to kraut!
And after, there were grapes that hid their brightness under
　　a gray dust,
Then gushed thrilling, purple blood over the fire;
And enamelled crab-apples that tricked with their fragrance
But were bitter to taste.
And there were spicy plums and ill-shaped quinces,
And long string-beans floating in pans of clear water
Like slim, green fishes.
And there was fish itself,
Salted, silver herring from the city. . . .

And you moved among these mysteries,
Absorbed and smiling and sure;
Stirring, tasting, measuring,
With the precision of a ritual.
I like to think of you in your years of power—
You, now so shaken and so powerless—
High priestess of your home.
　　　　　　　　　　　　JEAN STARR UNTERMEYER

PORTRAITS AND FANCIES

THE SHEPHERDESS

Alice Meynell is an English poet. Her husband, Wilfrid Meynell, is a well-known critic. Their kindness and the shelter of their home meant much to another English poet, Francis Thompson. Their daughter, Viola Meynell, is also a poet. Mrs. Meynell's sister, Lady Butler, is a well-known painter. Mrs. Meynell died in 1922.

"The Shepherdess" has the simplicity, the sincerity, and the individual diction that characterize the new poetry. The metaphor of the shepherdess is delicately and satisfyingly sustained throughout.

She walks—the lady of my delight—
A shepherdess of sheep.
Her flocks are thoughts. She keeps them white;
She guards them from the steep.
She feeds them on the fragrant height,
And folds them in for sleep.

She roams maternal hills and bright,
Dark valleys safe and deep.
Her dreams are innocent at night;
The chastest stars may peep.
She walks—the lady of my delight—
A shepherdess of sheep.

She holds her little thoughts in sight,
Though gay they run and leap.
She is so circumspect and right;
She has her soul to keep.
She walks—the lady of my delight—
A shepherdess of sheep.

ALICE MEYNELL

ANNE RUTLEDGE

Edgar Lee Masters was born in Kansas. He was educated at
Knox College, Galesburg, Illinois. He is a successful lawyer,
interested in politics. He is a member of the National Institute
of Arts and Letters. Besides his famous "Spoon River Anthology" he has published several volumes of poetry.

"Anne Rutledge" and "Isaiah Beethoven" are from the
"Spoon River Anthology," one of the strangest and most startling books of modern times. Amy Lowell calls it "the epic of
every-day life." In it the people buried in a small-town cemetery
put to shame the inscriptions on their gravestones by insisting
on telling the truth about themselves and their neighbors. We
re-create not only the village but the graveyard, where lichens
blacken the stones, and weeds and nettles thrive in neglected
corners. But as in such spots a few lilies and clumps of phlox
and spice-pinks bloom year after year, so some of the dead pro-
claim messages of beauty and well-ordered lives.

Anne Rutledge was the young girl whom Abraham Lincoln
loved, and lost through death. Isaiah Beethoven was the man
who, with three months to live, learned the lesson of immortality from the river and saw at last

> "a flash of trumpets
> Above the battlements over Time!"

Out of me unworthy and unknown
The vibrations of deathless music;
"With malice toward none, with charity for all."
Out of me the forgiveness of millions toward millions,
And the beneficent face of a nation
Shining with justice and truth.
I am Anne Rutledge who sleep beneath these weeds,
Beloved in life of Abraham Lincoln,
Wedded to him, not through union,
But through separation.
Bloom forever, O Republic,
From the dust of my bosom!

                                        EDGAR LEE MASTERS

ISAIAH BEETHOVEN

They told me I had three months to live,
So I crept to Bernadotte,
And sat by the mill for hours and hours
Where the gathered waters deeply moving
Seemed not to move:
O world, that's you!
You are but a widened place in the river
Where Life looks down and we rejoice for her
Mirrored in us, and so we dream
And turn away, but when again
We look for the face, behold the lowlands
And blasted cottonwood trees where we empty
Into the larger stream!
But here by the mill the castled clouds
Mocked themselves in the dizzy water;
And over its agate floor at night
The flame of the moon ran under my eyes
Amid a forest stillness broken
By a flute in a hut on the hill.
At last when I came to lie in bed
Weak and in pain, with the dreams about me,
The soul of the river had entered my soul,
And the gathered power of my soul was moving
So swiftly it seemed to be at rest
Under cities of cloud and under
Spheres of silver and changing worlds—
Until I saw a flash of trumpets
Above the battlements over Time!

                              EDGAR LEE MASTERS

A LADY

Amy Lowell, born at Brookline, was a member of the famous Lowell family of Massachusetts. She was educated by private tutors and by travel. For eight years she published nothing while she served a self-imposed apprenticeship to her art. She was an Imagist poet and a writer of *vers libre* and polyphonic prose. She takes high rank among modern poetic critics. Her death occurred soon after the publication of her biography of Keats, in 1925.

In a book of this size it is impossible to do justice to Amy Lowell. She was an Imagist, but she was surely more than that. "A Lady," however, illustrates her ideas of what a poem should be: "A clear presentation of whatever the author wishes to convey," and "patterned effects of rhyme and metre, brevity, and conciseness."

> You are beautiful and faded,
> Like an old opera tune
> Played upon a harpsichord;
> Or like the sun-flooded silks
> Of an eighteenth century boudoir.
> In your eyes
> Smoulder the fallen roses of outlived minutes,
> And the perfume of your soul
> Is vague and suffusing,
> With the pungence of sealed spice jars.
> Your half-tones delight me,
> And I grow mad with gazing
> At your blent colors.
>
> My vigor is a new-minted penny,
> Which I cast at your feet.
> Gather it up from the dust,
> That its sparkle may amuse you.
>   AMY LOWELL

MISS LOO

For the biography of Walter de la Mare, see "Silver."
The gift of portraiture, as well as many other gifts, belongs to
Walter de la Mare. Each of us has in mind some one whose
personality is unforgettable—often some one associated with
our childhood. As in the case of "Miss Loo," the picture is composed of many details of environment, feature, and manner—
details which an artist like de la Mare can combine into a perfect likeness.

When thin-strewn memory I look through,
I see most clearly poor Miss Loo,
Her tabby-cat, her cage of birds,
Her nose, her hair—her muffled words,
And how she'd open her green eyes,
As if in some immense surprise,
Whenever as we sat at tea
She made some small remark to me.

It's always drowsy summer when
From out the past she comes again;
The westering sunshine in a pool
Floats in her parlor still and cool;
While the slim bird its lean wire shakes,
As into piercing song it breaks,
Till Peter's pale-green eyes ajar
Dream, wake; wake, dream, in one brief bar.

And I am sitting, dull and shy,
And she with gaze of vacancy,
And large hands folded on the tray,
Musing the afternoon away;
Her satin bosom heaving slow

With sighs that softly ebb and flow,
And her plain face in such dismay,
It seems unkind to look her way:
Until all cheerful back will come
Her cheerful gleaming spirit home:
And one would think that poor Miss Loo
Asked nothing else, if she had you.

WALTER DE LA MARE

POCAHONTAS

Vachel Lindsay was born at Springfield, Illinois. He was educated at Hiram College, Ohio, and at the Chicago Art Institute.
He also studied in the New York School of Art, under Chase
and Henri. He lectured for the Y. M. C. A. and the Anti-Saloon
League. Later he walked from Illinois to New Mexico, trading
his poems for meals and lodging. He has published three volumes
of prose, besides his books of poetry.

The rhythmic plan of this poem is less daring than that of
many of Mr. Lindsay's poems. It is suited to the dignity and
the quiet of the subject, and its regularity is relieved by short
lines which suggest the arresting sounds of nature in the forest
in the spring.

> Her skin was rosy copper-red,
> And high she held her beauteous head.
> Her step was like a rustling leaf;
> Her heart a nest, untouched of grief.
> She dreamed of sons like Powhatan,
> And through her blood the lightning ran.
> Love-cries with the birds she sung,
> Birdlike
> In the grape-vine swung.
> The Forest, arching low and wide,
> Gloried in its Indian bride.
>
> Rolfe, that dim adventurer,
> Had not come a courtier.
> John Rolfe is not our ancestor.
> We rise from out the soul of her
> Held in native wonderland
> While the sun's rays kissed her hand,
> In the springtime,
> In Virginia,
> Our Mother, Pocahontas.

VACHEL LINDSAY

THE OLD WOMAN

Joseph Campbell was born at Belfast, Ireland. He is an illustrator by profession, and has illustrated one volume of his own verse. He writes for Irish and American magazines. Many of his verses are published under the Gaelic form of his name (Seosamh MacCathmhaoil).

"The Old Woman" is a fine illustration of symbolism. The austerity of the poem is notable; not a word, not a line too much. Yet the picture is perfect.

As a white candle
　In a holy place,
So is the beauty
　Of an agèd face.

As the spent radiance
　Of the winter sun,
So is a woman
　With her travail done.

Her brood gone from her,
　And her thoughts as still
As the waters
　Under a ruined mill.

JOSEPH CAMPBELL

WHEN THE YEAR GROWS OLD

Edna St. Vincent Millay was born in Rockport, Maine. She is a graduate of Vassar. She has written much poetry of fine quality and several plays.

A great artist sometimes paints a masterpiece to which he gives only the simple title, "Portrait of a Lady." "When the Year Grows Old" is such a portrait in words of one who loved summer skies and dreaded winter's cold as might an entrapped butterfly or a tropical bird. The portrait effect is secured by well-chosen details.

I cannot but remember
   When the year grows old—
October—November—
   How she disliked the cold!

She used to watch the swallows
   Go down across the sky,
And turn from the window
   With a little sharp sigh.

And often when the brown leaves
   Were brittle on the ground,
And the wind in the chimney
   Made a melancholy sound,

She had a look about her
   That I wish I could forget—
The look of a scared thing
   Sitting in a net!

Oh, beautiful at nightfall
   The soft spitting snow!

And beautiful the bare boughs
　　Rubbing to and fro!

But the roaring of the fire,
　　And the warmth of fur,
And the boiling of the kettle
　　Were beautiful to her!

I cannot but remember
　　When the year grows old—
October—November—
　　How she disliked the cold!

EDNA ST. VINCENT MILLAY

MINIVER CHEEVY

For a biographical sketch of Edwin Arlington Robinson, see
"The House on the Hill."

"Miniver Cheevy" is one of a number of Mr. Robinson's fine
word-portraits. An Imagist, he uses the exact word, the clear
image. His reticence suggests the sparing tendencies of New
England. While it is Miniver Cheevy who sits for a verbal portrait, the author has somehow drawn, in the background, Miniver's practical, unimaginative neighbors, who no doubt scorned
his passion for the mediæval.

Miniver Cheevy, child of scorn,
 Grew lean while he assailed the seasons;
He wept that he was ever born,
 And he had reasons.

Miniver loved the days of old
 When swords were bright and steeds were prancing;
The vision of a warrior bold
 Would set him dancing.

Miniver sighed for what was not,
 And dreamed, and rested from his labors;
He dreamed of Thebes and Camelot,
 And Priam's neighbors.

Miniver mourned the ripe renown
 That made so many a name so fragrant;
He mourned Romance, now on the town,
 And Art, a vagrant.

Miniver loved the Medici,
 Albeit he had never seen one;

He would have sinned incessantly
  Could he have been one.

Miniver cursed the commonplace
  And eyed a khaki suit with loathing;
He missed the mediæval grace
  Of iron clothing.

Miniver scorned the gold he sought,
  But sore annoyed was he without it;
Miniver thought, and thought, and thought,
  And thought about it.

Miniver Cheevy, born too late,
  Scratched his head and kept on thinking;
Miniver coughed, and called it fate,
  And kept on drinking.

EDWIN ARLINGTON ROBINSON

THE SLEEPING BEAUTY

Mary Carolyn Davies was born at Sprague, Washington. She studied at the University of California and the University of New York. She won two prizes for poetry while in college and was one of the founders of "Others," a group of writers of free verse. In 1919 she was adopted as a member of the Blackfoot Indian tribe and given the name of Pawtuskie (Pine Woman).

"The Sleeping Beauty" deals with an old story in a new way. Its words and details are "sleepy" words and "sleepy" details. The time effect and the "return" are good.

The princess sleeps
   And her hair grows long.
And her birds sleep
   Each with a song
Stuck in his throat;
   And over her bower,
   Hour after hour,
The buds sleep too.

The old cook sleeps.
   And the quiet braids
   Of the serving maids
Are gold in the sun.
   And in the yard
   The knights that guard
Sleep every one;
   And, near the throne
The captains tall
Are sleeping all
   As though cut in stone;
Each cardinal

Sleeps; and the king
And the queen, with a ring
Of pages round.

And the world spins round.
And the princess sleeps.

Thrust after tnrust
A prince hews strong—
At the hedge, and his hair
And his face are fair.
(He is not the man
Who will waken the princess,
His eyes will be gone
And his bones will lie
And catch the light
When the prince rides by
Whose kiss will stir
The world and her.
He is only one
Of the hundred men
Who will dream of the princess,
Die, and then
Be a pathway white
For the last brave knight
To lead him straight
Where her lips await.)
And he sings
As he feels the stings
Of the thorns,
And he cries
To his page
"Courage, lad!

Hew on and thrust,
If God is just
　We shall wake her
　And take her
Home to our kingdom.
You will be squire to her,
Walk at her bridle—
　She will be smiling
　And speaking out shyly
All that her heart holds,
　And singing a little
　For gladness of waking.
And I shall make Life
　Bow on its knees to her;
　· I shall make Life
　Bow on its knees to her;—
Hew on and thrust;
If God is just,
　We shall find her
　And wake her
　And take her home."

In its iron hands
　For the miles around
A silence keeps
The forest deeps.
　And the world spins round.
—And the princess sleeps.

MARY CAROLYN DAVIES

A WHITE IRIS

Pauline B. Barrington is known to us only through this poem, permission to use which was obtained through Samuel Travers Clover, himself a writer and a newspaper man. He is now editor of the *Argonaut*, published at Los Angeles.

Tall and clothed in samite,
Chaste and pure,
In smooth armor,—
Your head held high
In its helmet
Of silver:
Jean D'Arc riding
Among the sword blades!

Has Spring for you
Wrought visions,
As it did for her
In a garden?   PAULINE B. BARRINGTON

LADDIES

Edgar A. Guest was born in England. He came to the United States when he was ten years old. He has been connected with the Detroit *Free Press* since 1895. In this paper he conducts a column of verse and humorous sketches. His verses are syndicated throughout the country and have been published in a number of volumes.

Show me the boy who never threw
A stone at some one's cat,
Or never hurled a snowball swift
At some one's high silk hat—
Who never ran away from school,
To seek the swimming-hole,
Or slyly from a neighbor's yard
Green apples never stole—

Show me the boy who never broke
A pane of window glass,
Who never disobeyed the sign
That says: "Keep off the grass."
Who never did a thousand things,
That grieve us sore to tell,
And I'll show you a little boy
Who must be far from well.

EDGAR A. GUEST

THE FECKENHAM MEN

For the biographical sketch of John Drinkwater, see "In Lady Street."

"The Feckenham Men" is a gay little poem which preaches a sermon on the value of beauty; not that the writer would have us destroy beans to gather blossoms! It reminds us of the philosophy of the Persian poet Saadi, who wrote:

> "If of thy mortal goods thou art bereft,
>   And from thy slender store two loaves alone are left,
>   Sell one and with the dole
>   Buy hyacinths to feed thy soul."

The jolly men at Feckenham
Don't count their goods as common men,
Their heads are full of silly dreams
From half-past ten to half-past ten,
They'll tell you why the stars are bright,
And some sheep black and some sheep white.

The jolly men at Feckenham
Draw wages of the sun and rain,
And count as good as golden coin
The blossoms on the window-pane,
And Lord! they love a sinewy tale
Told over pots of foaming ale.

Now here's a tale of Feckenham
Told to me by a Feckenham man,
Who, being only eighty years,
Ran always when the red fox ran,
And looked upon the earth with eyes
As quiet as unclouded skies.

These jolly men of Feckenham
One day when summer strode in power
Went down, it seems, among their lands
And saw their bean-fields all in flower—
"Wheat-ricks," they said, "be good to see;
What would a rick of blossoms be?"

So straight they brought their sickles out
And worked all day till day was done,
And builded them a good square rick
Of scented bloom beneath the sun.
And was not this I tell to you
A fiery-hearted thing to do?

JOHN DRINKWATER

THE FIDDLER OF DOONEY

For the biographical sketch of William Butler Yeats, see "The Song of Wandering Aengus."

"The Fiddler of Dooney" is characteristic of reverent Irish daring where things of the soul are concerned. The Irish fiddler, like the Irish story-teller, believes in the importance, even the sacredness, of his calling.

When I play on my fiddle in Dooney
Folk dance like a wave of the sea;
My cousin is priest in Kilvarnet,
My brother in Moharabuiee.

I passed my brother and cousin:
They read in their books of prayer;
I read in my book of songs
I bought at the Sligo fair.

When we come at the end of time,
To Peter sitting in state,
He will smile on the three old spirits,
But call me first through the gate.

For the good are always the merry,
Save by an evil chance,
And the merry love the fiddle
And the merry love to dance.

And when the folk there spy me,
They will come up to me,
With "Here is the fiddler of Dooney!"
And dance like a wave of the sea.

WILLIAM BUTLER YEATS

THE SONG OF WANDERING AENGUS

William Butler Yeats is probably the most famous living Irish poet. He was born in Sligo, Ireland, and educated at the Godolphin School, Hammersmith, England, and at the Erasmus Smith School in Dublin. With Lady Gregory he founded the Irish National Theatre, later known as the Abbey Theatre. His collected poems make eight volumes. He has published many plays, of which the best-beloved is "The Land of Heart's Desire."

"The Song of Wandering Aengus" is based on one of the legends of Ireland, that of the divine children of Danu, who long, long ago came to Ireland. They have the power to take any shape, and those that haunt the waters of Ireland often disguise themselves as fish. If a fisherman wants to protect himself against them, he takes with him a drop of holy water and a pinch of salt. This poem describes in simple fashion and in simple diction the spell which one of these "glimmering girls" worked upon the fisherman. The number of monosyllabic words is remarkable.

I went out to the hazel wood
Because a fire was in my head,
And cut and peeled a hazel wand,
And hooked a berry to a thread;
And when white moths were on the wing,
And moth-like stars were flickering out,
I dropped the berry in a stream,
And caught a little silver trout.

When I had laid it on the floor,
I went to blow the fire a-flame,
But something rustled on the floor,
And some one called me by my name:
It had become a glimmering girl,
With apple-blossom in her hair,
Who called me by my name and ran
And faded through the brightening air.

Though I am old with wandering
Through hollow lands and hilly lands,
I will find out where she has gone,
And kiss her lips and take her hands;
And walk among long dappled grass,
And pluck till time and times are done
The silver apples of the moon,
The golden apples of the sun.

WILLIAM BUTLER YEATS

I AM IN LOVE WITH HIGH FAR–SEEING PLACES

For the biography of Arthur Davison Ficke, see "I Am
Weary of Being Bitter"

I am in love with high far-seeing places
That look on plains half-sunlight and half-storm,
In love with hours when from the circling faces
Veils pass, and laughing fellowship glows warm.
You who look on me with grave eyes where rapture
And April love of living burn confessed—
The gods are good! the world lies free to capture!
Life has no walls. Oh, take me to your breast!
Take me—be with me for a moment's span!
I am in love with all unveiled faces
I seek the wonder at the heart of man;
I would go up to the far-seeing places.
While youth is ours, turn toward me for a space
The marvel of your rapture-lighted face!

ARTHUR DAVISON FICKE

THE ORPHANS

For the biographical sketch of Wilfrid Wilson Gibson, see "The Lonely Tree."

"The Orphans" is in Mr. Gibson's lighter vein, but just as exact and forceful in diction as his war poems are.

At five o'clock one April morn
I met them making tracks,
Young Benjamin and Abel Horn,
With bundles on their backs.

Young Benjamin is seventy-five,
Young Abel, seventy-seven—
The oldest innocents alive
Beneath that April heaven.

I asked them why they trudged about
With crabby looks and sour—
"And does your mother know you're out
At this unearthly hour?"

They stopped: and scowling up at me,
Each shook a grizzled head,
And swore; and then spat bitterly,
As with one voice they said:

"Homeless, about the country-side
We never thought to roam;
But mother, she has gone and died,
And broken up the home."

WILFRID WILSON GIBSON

HER WORDS

Anna Hempstead Branch was born in New London, Connecticut. She was educated at the Adelphi Academy, Brooklyn, at Smith College, and at the American Academy of Dramatic Art. She won the first *Century* prize for the best poem of the year written by a college graduate. She is the author of a successful play and of a number of volumes of poetry.

The importance of words, on which the new poetry so strongly insists, is here beautifully illustrated by the theme as well as by the diction of the author.

My mother has the prettiest tricks
  Of words and words and words.
Her talk comes out as smooth and sleek
  As breasts of singing birds.

She shapes her speech all silver fine
  Because she loves it so.
And her own eyes begin to shine
  To hear her stories grow.

And if she goes to make a call
  Or out to take a walk,
We leave our work when she returns
  And run to hear her talk.

We had not dreamed these things were so
  Of sorrow and of mirth.
Her speech is as a thousand eyes
  Through which we see the earth.

God wove a web of loveliness,
  Of clouds and stars and birds,

But made not anything at all
    So beautiful as words.

They shine around our simple earth
    With golden shadowings,
And every common thing they touch
    Is exquisite with wings.

There's nothing poor and nothing small
    But is made fair with them.
They are the hands of living faith
    That touch the garment's hem.

They are as fair as bloom or air,
    They shine like any star,
And I am rich who learned from her
    How beautiful they are.

ANNA HEMPSTEAD BRANCH

SONG AGAINST CHILDREN

Aline Kilmer was born at Norfolk, Virginia. She was educated at the Rutgers Preparatory School and at the Vail-Deane
School, both in New Jersey. She was the wife of Joyce Kilmer,
who was killed in the World War. Her poems about children
are especially fine.

The gay charm of this and other songs about children by
Mrs. Kilmer makes us sure that she must be a delightful com-
panion. The repetition in the poem is a feature that children,
big and little, love.

O the barberry bright, the barberry bright!
It stood on the mantelpiece because of the height.
Its stems were slender and thorny and tall
And it looked most beautiful against the gray wall.
But Michael climbed up there in spite of the height
And he ate all the berries off the barberry bright.

O the round holly wreath, the round holly wreath!
It hung in the window with ivy beneath.
It was plump and prosperous, spangled with red,
And I thought it would cheer me although I were dead.
But Deborah climbed on a table beneath
And she ate all the berries off the round holly wreath

O the mistletoe bough, the mistletoe bough!
Could any one touch it? I didn't see how.
I hung it up high that it might last long,
I wreathed it with ribbons and hailed it with song.
But Christopher reached it, I do not know how,
And he ate all the berries off the mistletoe bough.

                                        ALINE KILMER

RED SLIPPERS

For the biographical sketch of Amy Lowell, see "A Lady."
"Red Slippers" is an example of polyphonic prose. Miss
Lowell tells us in "Tendencies of Modern American Poetry"
that "polyphonic" means "many-voiced" and "the form is so
called because it makes use of all the 'voices' of poetry, viz.:
metre, vers libre, assonance, alliteration, rhyme, and return."
"Red Slippers" should be read aloud to catch its cadences and
rhymes. The colors are described so accurately that we seem
to be looking into the shop window with her and verifying all
the effects she mentions. And in the sweep of the poem there
is something that excites us and hurries us on.

Red slippers in a shop-window; and outside in the street,
flaws of gray, windy sleet!

Behind the polished glass the slippers hang in long threads
of red, festooning from the ceiling like stalactites of blood,
flooding the eyes of passers-by with dripping color, jamming
their crimson reflections against the windows of cabs and
tram-cars, screaming their claret and salmon into the teeth
of the sleet, plopping their little round maroon lights upon
the tops of umbrellas.

The row of white, sparkling shop-fronts is gashed and
bleeding, it bleeds red slippers. They spout under the electric light, fluid and fluctuating, a hot rain—and freeze again
to red slippers, myriadly multiplied in the mirror side of the
window.

They balance upon arched insteps like springing bridges of
crimson lacquer; they swing up over curved heels like whirl-
ing tanagers sucked in a wind-pocket; they flatten out, heel-
less, like July ponds, flared and burnished by red rockets.

Snap, snap, they are cracker sparks of scarlet in the white, monotonous block of shops.

They plunge the clangor of billions of vermilion trumpets into the crowd outside, and echo in faint rose over the pavement.

People hurry by, for these are only shoes, and in a window farther down is a big lotus bud of cardboard, whose petals open every few minutes and reveal a wax doll, with staring bead eyes and flaxen hair, lolling awkwardly in its flower chair.

One has often seen shoes, but whoever saw a cardboard lotus bud before?

The flaws of gray, windy sleet beat on the shop-window where there are only red slippers.

AMY LOWELL

WON BY EAR

Daniel W. Troy is a lawyer and a poet. He lives in Montgom-
ery, Alabama. He writes for well-known magazines.

In this day of syncopated music, "Won by Ear" is sure t
do what Mr. Troy hopes it will, "help some kid to laugh."

Theah's a man up the street
Ah'm jus' itchin' tuh meet—
He's the man with the slidin' trombone.
Ah don't understan'
How he does it so gran'
But he sho' gits uh wonderful tone.
That Mendels'n Song—
He jus' rags it uh-long
An' zoons it right intuh mah soul.
When he plays "Ovuh Theah"
Ev'ry kink in mah haih
Jus' natchully stahts tuh unroll.
Mistah Man, Mistah Honey,
Take me an' mah money,
Whenevuh yo' wants me Ah'm yo'n.
Ah'll cook while you eat—
Shine the shoes on yo' feet—
If yo'll play on that slidin' trombone.

DANIEL W. TROY

THE FISHERMAN'S TAX

[*Time about the Sixth or Seventh Century A. D.*]

For the biographical sketch of Grace Shoup, see "The Vase."

The Landsman Speaks

Oh, fortunate are the fishermen,
  And a happy folk are ye,
For the tax that grinds all the poor alike,
  Never touches the men of the sea.

The Fisherman Answers

Ah! well you know in your landsman's heart,
  You'd pay the dues for four,
Or ever you'd rise at the dead of night,
  When the ghosts tap on the door.

Yours is a tax of the copper coin,
  But ours is a tax of dread—
To rise at night in the faint moonlight,
  To ferry the voiceless dead.

But a week agone, it fell my turn,
  And the fishermen said to me,
"*Brother, look well to-night when you take
  The dead men over the sea.*"

My mother she cried the livelong eve,
  Till a sound came out in the dark,
And a muffled tap on the half-closed door
  Made even the children hark.

And I rose and followed through the night
  A spot of dark and shine,
That might be either a form of dread
  Or a gleam of light on the brine.

We came to my boat on the waterside;
  I knew the place to stand,
For with dark forms that I could not see
  'Twas crowded on every hand.

The boat sunk low in the water lay—
  How strange it seemed to me,
To think the dead no man could see
  Should yet so heavy be!

And strange it was in the thick, sad night,
  With the dark waves rolling on,
And the face of the moon, so pale and white,
  As it shone once and was gone.

And the seals raised up their round wet heads,
  And the mermaids chanted low;
But I durst not look to the left or right,
  I durst but bend and row.

Six days it takes to cross the tide
  'Twixt here and Britain's Isle;
I rowed one night and the task seemed light,
  But the ghosts they helped the while.

For ever they held a spot of light
  Up over the darkness' head,
And ever after that spot of light,
  Our boat so swiftly sped.

The dawn of day was on its way
   When we reached the dead men's shore,
At the dead men's call, they started all,
   And my boat floated free once more.

But my wife and babes and mother old,
   Wept and watched through the night;
'Twas only their prayers that brought me back
   Again by the morning light.

Said I not right, ye landsmen friends,
   Much taxes ye would pay,
Ere ye would ferry the dead across
   To their isle by break of day?

GRACE SHOUP

"The fishermen on the Gaulish coast were made the ferrymen of the dead; and on account of their strange duty, we are assured, they were exempt from the ordinary incidence of taxation."
—Keary's "Vikings in Western Christendom."

HAUNTED

Wilbert Snow was born in Maine. He has been a sailor before
the mast, a Klondike miner, a lieutenant in the World War
and a teacher of English in half a dozen American universities.
He is now a professor of English in Connecticut Wesleyan. He
is the author of "Maine Coast," a book of poems dealing with
the folk of his native shores.

There are strange noises around an old house at midnight,
Where our minds are most awake.
Are they the forgotten owners coming back to make them-
    selves felt,
And throw off the oblivion to which we have so carelessly
    consigned them?

The shutters make a breathing sound
As if some faithful hired man
Had come back, and was using them for lungs.

A faint tinkle, as of iron, floats up from the cellar.
Is it the stirring of a former tenant
Trying to shake off death's chains?

A rooster calls out loudly two hours before his time.
I imagine he is greeting his old master
Who is rustling the leaves
Walking among the hollyhocks by the garden wall.

A bubble of earth resounds far off,
Like the removal of a bung from a cask of old wine.
Is it the echo from one of earth's haunted places,
Opened to let ghosts wander free?

The floor creaks insistently overhead.
Perhaps it is some spirit walking in the attic
To see if his childhood playthings are still there.

There is a wailing in the wind
Around the corner of the house,—
A wailing as of the crying of gulls,
Or the sighing of children who have been whipped and sent
to bed hungry.

Is this a sighing protest against being sent to the bed of
death,
When earth itself is so lovely?

What are these strange noises that cluster around an old
house at midnight?

WILBERT SNOW

THE LISTENERS

For Walter de la Mare's biography, see "Silver."

Moonlight, a forest, a lonely old house untenanted except by its own dreams of human life, a traveller who knocks loudly and talks in every-day language, a restless horse which makes uneasy noises as it champs "the grasses of the forest's ferny floor"—all combine to make a wonderful poem and a thrilling ghost story.

Alden tells us in "An Introduction to Poetry" that Chopin is said to have kept perfect time with his left hand when he was playing his waltzes, but to have used with his right hand what musicians call "stolen time." Whether Chopin really did this has been disputed; but such a device appears in "The Listeners." The opening line has the effect of one talking; the second line is a familiar rhythm. So throughout there are regular departures from the conventional rhythm and regular returns to it. The effect is new and charming. The conventional rhythm satisfies by its familiarity; the unusual rhythm prevents monotony.

"Is there anybody there?" said the Traveller,
    Knocking on the moonlit door;
And his horse in the silence champed the grasses
    Of the forest's ferny floor;
And a bird flew up out of the turret,
    Above the Traveller's head;
And he smote upon the door again a second time;
    "Is there anybody there?" he said.
But no one descended to the Traveller;
    No head from the leaf-fringed sill
Leaned over and looked into his gray eyes,
    Where he stood perplexed and still.
But only a host of phantom listeners
    That dwelt in the lone house then
Stood listening in the quiet of the moonlight
    To that voice from the world of men:
Stood thronging the faint moonbeams on the dark stair,

That goes down to the empty hall,
Hearkening in an air stirred and shaken
  By the lonely Traveller's call.
And he felt in his heart their strangeness,
  Their stillness answering his cry,
While his horse moved, cropping the dark turf,
  'Neath the starred and leafy sky;
For he suddenly smote on the door, even
  Louder, and lifted his head:—
"Tell them I came, and no one answered;
  That I kept my word," he said.
Never the least stir made the listeners,
  Though every word he spake
Fell echoing through the shadowiness of the still house
  From the one man left awake:
Ay, they heard his foot upon the stirrup,
  And the sound of iron on stone,
And how the silence surged softly backward,
  When the plunging hoofs were gone.

                       WALTER DE LA MARE

DAPHNE

Hildegarde Flanner was born in Indianapolis. She was educated in Shortridge High School of Indianapolis and at the University of California. She has published "Mansions," a one-act
play, and several volumes of poetry. The most recent is "A
Tree in Bloom." She lives in Pasadena, California.

"Daphne" is a legend to which the writer has imparted charm
by fortunate diction, unusual figures, and delicate reticences.

> They told her she had hair the color
> Of a nightingale.
> They told her that her eyes were candles
> Lit beneath a veil.
>
> They praised her feet like narrow doves
> Mated on the floor,
> Saying there were never feet
> Like her feet before.
>
> They praised her shining voice that rang
> Like stars dropped in a glass.
> "Sing to thy little yellow shell!"
> And so the night would pass.
>
> But when they came too near to her
> And touched her with the hand,
> She drew her hair across her eyes.
> She could not understand.
>
> And when they said a thing to her
> That she had never heard,
> Her heart plunged into silence there
> Like a hunted bird.

She caught her violet mantle close,
The Tyrian upon the white.
She quivered like a little twig.
She stepped into the night.

They called her name within the dark,
They searched beneath the sun,
But there was not a broken flower
To show where she had run.

Everything was very still,
Far too still, they said.
So they turned and went away
Unaccompanied.

Nothing moved where they had sought,
Nothing sang or wept.
Beneath the tree that had no name,
Silence turned and slept.

HILDEGARDE FLANNER

AT THE AQUARIUM

For the biographical sketch of Max Eastman, see "Coming to
Port."

Serene the silver fishes glide,
Stern-lipped, and pale, and wonder-eyed!
As through the aged deeps of ocean,
They glide with wan and wavy motion!
They have no pathway where they go.
They flow like water to and fro.
They watch with never-winking eyes,
They watch with staring, cold surprise,
The level people in the air,
The people peering, peering there:
Who wander also to and fro,
And know not why or where they go,
Yet have a wonder in their eyes,
Sometimes a pale and cold surprise.

MAX EASTMAN

AS I CAME DOWN FROM LEBANON

Clinton Scollard was born in Clinton, New York. He was educated at Hamilton College, at Harvard, and at Cambridge, England. He is the author of a number of volumes of poetry and much excellent magazine verse. He is a member of the National Institute of Arts and Letters. He married Jessie B. Rittenhouse in 1924.

"As I Came Down from Lebanon" is characterized by the smooth beauty of its lines, its glowing colors, and its atmosphere of the East and the desert.

As I came down from Lebanon,
Came winding, wandering slowly down
Through mountain passes bleak and brown,
The cloudless day was well-nigh done.
The city, like an opal set
In emerald, showed each minaret
Afire with radiant beams of sun,
And glistened orange, fig, and lime,
Where song-birds made melodious chime,
As I came down from Lebanon.

As I came down from Lebanon,
Like lava in the dying glow,
Through olive orchards far below
I saw the murmuring river run;
And 'neath the wall upon the sand
Swart sheiks from distant Samarcand,
With precious spices they had won,
Lay long and languidly in wait
Till they might pass the guarded gate,
As I came down from Lebanon.

As I came down from Lebanon,
I saw strange men from lands afar,
In mosque and square and gay bazaar,
The Magi that the Moslem shun,
And grave Effendi from Stamboul,
Who sherbet sipped in corners cool;
And, from the balconies o'errun
With roses, gleamed the eyes of those
Who dwell in still seraglios,
As I came down from Lebanon.

As I came down from Lebanon,
The flaming flower of daytime died,
And Night, arrayed as is a bride
Of some great king, in garments spun
Of purple and the finest gold,
Out-bloomed in glories manifold,
Until the moon, above the dun
And darkening desert, void of shade,
Shone like a keen Damascus blade.
As I came down from Lebanon.

CLINTON SCOLLARD

SHEEP

For the biographical sketch of Carl Sandburg, see "Fog."

Thousands of sheep, soft-footed, black-nosed sheep—one by one going up the hill and over the fence—one by one four-footed pattering up and over—one by one wiggling their stub tails as they take the short jump and go over—one by one silently unless for the multitudinous drumming of their hoofs as they move on and go over—thousands and thousands of them in the gray haze of evening just after sundown —one by one slanting in a long line to pass over the hill.—

I am the slow, long-legged Sleepyman and I love you, sheep in Persia, California, Argentine, Australia, or Spain— you are my thoughts that help me when I, the Sleepyman, lay my hands on the eyelids of the children of the world at eight o'clock every night—you thousands and thousands of sheep in a procession of dusk making an endless multitudinous drumming on the hills with your hoofs.

CARL SANDBURG

TO THINK

Elizabeth J. Coatsworth was born in Buffalo, New York. She is a graduate of Vassar and has travelled much in Europe and the Orient. The impressions of much early travel have lent color to her poetry.

To think I once saw grocery shops
With but a casual eye
And fingered figs and apricots
As one who came to buy.

To think I never dreamed of how
Bananas sway in rain
And often looked at oranges
And never thought of Spain.

And in those wasted days I saw
No sails above the tea,
For grocery shops were grocery shops—
Not hemispheres to me.

ELIZABETH J. COATSWORTH

COLOGNE CATHEDRAL

For the biographical sketch of Frances Shaw, see "The Harp of the Wind."

"Cologne Cathedral" gives us not only clear images but an architectural suggestion. The Gothic cathedrals are ornamented with gargoyles, hideous figures probably intended to frighten away evil spirits. Mrs. Shaw says, "Looking at the carved belfry, I saw out there a flock of real birds—probably the spirits of the carven gargoyles."

The little white prayers
    Of Elspeth Fry
Float up the arches
    Into the sky.

A little black bird
    On the belfry high
Pecks at them
    As they go by.

FRANCES SHAW

A MELANCHOLY BEAVER

Arthur Guiterman was born of American parentage in Vienna, Austria. He is a graduate of the College of the City of New York. He is noted for his humorous verse, of which he has published several volumes. Of late he has been writing a stirring series of ballads of American patriotism.

A melancholy Beaver
Resided by a rill;
He either had a fever
Or else he had a chill;

For Mental Inquisition
Had filled him full of dole
About his Earthly Mission
Or his eternal soul.

In June, instead of basking
Or helping build the dam,
He vexed his conscience, asking
"Why Is It That I Am?"

ARTHUR GUITERMAN

WISH

John Chipman Farrar was born at Burlington, Vermont. He served as first lieutenant in the United States Air Service, 1917-19. He is editor of *The Bookman* and author of three volumes of poetry.

A frog's a very happy thing,
Cool and green in early spring,
Quick and silver through the pool,
With no thoughts of books or school.

Oh, I want to be a frog—
Sunning, stretching on a log,
Blinking there in splendid ease,
Swimming naked when I please.

Nosing into magic nooks,
Quiet marshes, noisy brooks—
Free! and fit for anything—
Oh, to be a frog in spring!

JOHN CHIPMAN FARRAR

PARENTHOOD

For the biographical sketch of John Chipman Farrar, see
"Wish."

The birches that dance on the top of the hill
Are so slender and young that they cannot keep still.
They bend and they nod at each whiff of a breeze,
For you see they are still just the children of trees;

But the birches below in the valley are older,
They are calmer and straighter and taller and colder;
Perhaps when we've grown up as solemn and grave,
We, too, will have children that do not behave.

JOHN CHIPMAN FARRAR

INDEX OF AUTHORS

INDEX OF TITLES

INDEX OF FIRST LINES

15684